DAVID SHIELDS

BODY POLITIC

The Great American Sports Machine

Simon & Schuster

NEW YORK · LONDON · TORONTO · SYDNEY

SIMON & SCHUSTER
Rockefeller Center
1230 Avenue of the Americas
New York, NY 10020

SIMON & SCHUSTER and colophon are registered trademarks
of Simon & Schuster, Inc.

For information about special discounts for bulk purchases,
please contact Simon & Schuster Special Sales:
1-800-456-6798 or business@simonandschuster.com

Designed by Paul Dippolito

Manufactured in the United States of America

1   3   5   7   9   10   8   6   4   2

Library of Congress Cataloging-in-Publication Data
Shields, David.
Body politic: the great American sports machine / David Shields.
p.   cm.
1. Sports—Social aspects—United States.
2. Sports—United States—Psychological aspects. I. Title.
GV706.5.S53   2004
796'.0973—dc22   2004040190

ISBN 0-7432-4774-4

For the BWs

Thanks to Ted Miller for loaning me his tape; Peter Bailey, Jessica Burstein, Arne Christensen, Kris Coates, Roger Fanning, Christopher Potts, and Bailey Renner for many valuable suggestions; and especially to Michael Logan, whose often brilliant and always demanding responses were the very nearly daily adrenaline of the work.

CONTENTS

Fuck the game if it ain't sayin' nothin'.
—PUBLIC ENEMY

THE WOUND AND THE BOW
A Long Prologue

I KNOW THAT HOWARD COSELL WAS CHILDISHLY SELF-absorbed and petulant ("It's hard to describe the rage and frustration you feel, both personally and professionally, when you are vilified in a manner that would make Richard Nixon look like a beloved humanitarian. You can't imagine what it does to a person until you've experienced it yourself, especially when you know that the criticism is essentially unfair"); that he would obsess upon, say, the *Des Moines Register*'s critique of his performance; that too soon after he achieved prominence, the beautiful balance between righteous anger and comic self-importance got lost and he was left only with anger and self-importance; that he once said that he, along with Walter Cronkite and Johnny Carson, was one of the three great men in the history of American television; that he mercilessly teased his fellow *Monday Night Football* announc-

I

ers, Frank Gifford and Don Meredith, but pouted whenever they teased him; that he was certain he should have been a network anchor and/or a U.S. senator; that the very thing he thought needed deflating—the "importance of sports"—he was crucially responsible for inflating; that after hitching a ride on boxing and football for decades, he turned around and dismissed them when he no longer needed them ("The NFL has become a stagnant bore"; "I'm disgusted with the brutality of boxing"); that, in an attempt to assert his (nonexistent) expertise, he would frequently excoriate any rookie who had the temerity to commit an egregious error on *Monday Night Football* (dig the Cosellian diction); that he was a shameless name-dropper of people he barely knew; that he said about a black football player, "That little monkey gets loose," then, regarding the brouhaha that ensued, said, "They're conducting a literary pogrom against me"; that the *New York Times* sports columnist Red Smith once said, "I have tried hard to like Howard Cosell, and I have failed"; that the legendary sportswriter Jimmy Cannon said about him, "This is a guy who changed his name [from Cohane to Cosell], put on a toupee, and tried to convince the world he tells it like it is"; that David Halberstam said that Cosell bullied anyone who disagreed with him; that he frequently boasted about *Monday Night Football*, "We're bigger than the game"; that he once told a Senate subcommittee, "I'm a unique personality who has had more impact upon sports broadcasting in America than any person who has yet lived"; that he once wrote, "Who the hell made *Monday Night Football* unlike any other sports program on the air? If you want the plain truth, I did"; that at the height of his fame, when fans would come up to him on the street to kibitz or get an autograph, he liked to turn to whomever he was with and say (seriously? semi-seriously?), "Witness the adulation"; that when Gene Upshaw, the head of the NFL Players Association, said about Cosell, "His footprints are in the sand," Cosell corrected the compliment: "My footprints are cast in stone."

I know all that and don't really care, because during its first four years (1970–1973), when I was in high school, *Monday Night Football* mattered deeply to me and it mattered because of Cosell. I haven't watched more than a few minutes of any *MNF* game since then, and at the time, I had no very coherent sense of its significance, but looking back, I would say it's not an exaggeration to claim that Howard Cosell changed my life, maybe even—in at least one sense—saved it. *MNF* was "Mother Love's traveling freak show" (Meredith's weirdly perfect description), a "happening" (Cosell's revealingly unhip attempt to be hip); it was the first sports broadcast to feature three sportscasters, nine cameras, shotgun mics in the stands and up and down and around the field. Celebrities showed up in the booth: Nixon told Gifford that he wished he'd become a sportscaster instead of a politician; John Lennon told Cosell that he became a troublemaker because people didn't like his face (Cosell's comment afterward: "I know the feeling"); Cosell stood next to Bo Derek and said with pitch-perfect mock self-pity that here was a classic case of Beauty and the Beast; Cosell told John Wayne that he was a terrible singer, and the Duke agreed; after Cosell interviewed Spiro Agnew, Meredith said that what no one knew was that Agnew was wearing a Howard Cosell wristwatch. This was all cool and droll. It was all finally just showbiz, though. What wasn't was Cosell's relation, as an artist, to his material (I use the terms advisedly): "By standing parallel to the game and owing nothing to it, by demystifying it, by bullying it and not being bullied by it—by regarding the game as primarily an entertainment, though realizing also the social forces that impacted on it—I was able to turn *Monday Night Football* into an Event, and I do mean to use the capital E. Now it is part of American pop culture, and if it sounds like my ego is churning on overdrive for taking the lion's share of credit for it, then I'll take the mane."

I GREW UP in the '60s and '70s in suburban San Francisco, the son of left-wing Jewish journalist-activists. My mother was the public information officer for one of the first desegregated school districts in California. One day the human relations consultant informed her that the revolution wouldn't occur until white families gave up their houses in the suburbs and moved into the ghetto. My mother tried for the better part of the evening to convince us to put our house up for sale. One Easter weekend at Watts Towers, my mother looked smogward through some latticed wine bottles with a positively religious sparkle in her dark eyes. When my cousin Sarah married a black man from Philadelphia, Sarah's mother wasn't able to attend, so my mother substituted and brought the temple down with an a cappella finale of "Bridge Over Troubled Water." My father held dozens of jobs, but perhaps the one he loved the most was director of the San Mateo poverty program during the late '60s. He sat in a one-room office without central heating and called grocery stores, wanting to know why they didn't honor food stamps; called restaurants, asking if, as the sign in the window proclaimed, they were indeed equal-opportunity employers. Sometimes, on weekends, he flew to Sacramento or Washington to request more money for his program. Watts rioted; Detroit burned. My father said, "Please, I'm just doing my job." He got invited to barbecues, weddings, softball games. The salary was $7,500 a year, but I never saw him happier.

No one ever had his or her heart more firmly fixed in the right place than did my father and mother, with the possible exception of Howard Cosell. Traveling in a limo through a tough part of Kansas City on the way to the airport after a game, he saw two young black men fighting each other, surrounded by a group of guys cheering for blood. After telling his driver, Peggy, to stop the car, Cosell got out and instantaneously was the ringside announcer: "Now I want you to listen here. It's quite apparent to this observer that the young southpaw doesn't have a jab. And you, my friend, over here, you obviously do not have the stamina to continue. This conflict is halted posthaste." Handshakes, autographs. When Cosell got back in the limo and Peggy expressed her astonishment at what she'd just seen, Cosell leaned back, took a long drag on his cigar, and said, "Pegeroo, just remember one thing: I know who I am." Which, according to himself, was "a man of causes. My entire professional life has been predicated upon making the good fights, the fights that I believe in. And much of the time it was centered around the black athlete. My real fulfillment in broadcasting has always come from crusading journalism, fighting for the rights of people such as Jackie Robinson, Muhammad Ali, and Curt Flood. The greatest influence of my life was Jackie Roosevelt Robinson and [the inevitable namedrop] certainly one of my closest friends." My father rooted for the Dodgers because they were originally from Brooklyn and then moved to Los Angeles, just as he was and had, but we as a clan stayed loyal to them because they hired the major leagues' first black player (Jackie Robinson), retained the first crippled black player (Roy Campanella), and started the highest number of nice-seeming black players (Johnny Roseboro, Jim Gilliam, Tommy Davis, et al.). *New York Post* sportswriter Maury Allen said, "The single most significant issue in the twentieth-century was race, and Howard Cosell was unafraid about race."

Cosell's access to causes was through black bodies; without them, he wouldn't have been semi-dangerous, reviled. He defended Ali when the fighter refused to serve in Vietnam following his conversion to Islam. When Cosell died, Ali said, "Howard Cosell was a good man and he lived a good life. I can hear Howard now, saying, 'Muhammad, you're not the man you used to be ten years ago.'" Ali was referring to Cosell standing up at a prefight press conference and saying to him, "Many people believe you're not the man you used to be ten years ago." Ali had replied, "I spoke to your wife, and she said you're not the man you were *two* years ago." Cosell giggled like a schoolboy. Asked once what he stood for, Cosell said, "I stood for the Constitution, in the case of the U.S. versus Muhammad Ali. What the government did to this man was inhuman and illegal under the Fifth and Fourteenth amendments. Nobody says a damned word about the professional football players who dodged the draft. But Muhammad was different. He was black and he was boastful. Sportscasters today aren't concerned with causes and issues. Can you see any of those other guys putting their careers on the line for an Ali?" According to Cosell's daughter Jill, he frequently said that if people didn't stand for things, they weren't good for much else.

Music to my parents' Marxist ears. As was this: "The importance that our society attaches to sport is incredible. After all, is football a game or a religion? The people of this country have allowed sports to get completely out of hand." Or this: "The sports world is an ever-spinning spiral of deceit, immorality, absence of ethics, and defiance of the public interest." And this: "There's got to be a voice such as mine somewhere, and I enjoy poking my stick at various issues and passersby." And this: "For myself, I wondered when someone other than me would tell the truth." And this: "What was it all about, Alfie? Was football that important in this country? Was it a moral crime to introduce objective commentary to the transmission of a sports event?"— after he'd been pilloried in Cleveland for saying that Browns running back Leroy Kelly hadn't been a "compelling factor" in the first half of the first *MNF* game (he hadn't). "If so, how did we as a people get this way? In the spoon-fed, Alice in Wonderland world of sports broadcasting, the public was not accustomed to hearing its heroes questioned." When, following his eulogy of Bobby Kennedy on his *Speaking of Sports* show, fan after fan called in to complain ("Don't tell me how to live—just give us the scores—that's what you're paid for"), Cosell said, "I began to wonder if that kind of thinking is one of the things that makes us so prone to assassination in this country. Maybe there is such an absence of intellect and sensitivity that only violence is understandable and acceptable." "The 'fan,'" Cosell pointed out, "is a telephone worker, a transit worker, a power-company worker, a steelworker, a teacher, whatever. He has never given up the right to strike and often does. When he does, the public is inconvenienced and sometimes the public health and safety are threatened. When a ballplayer strikes, the effect upon the public health and safety is nil. Nor is public convenience disturbed, for that matter. Yet the ballplayer and the owner are called upon to each give up their individual bargaining rights because the 'fan' wants baseball and 'is entitled to get it.'" "I never played the game with advertisers, with my own company, or with the sports operators," Cosell said. "And of course, I never played the game as a professional athlete."

THIS IS WHERE it gets complicated, because I was a monomaniacal, 5' 4", 120-pound freshman basketball player at Aragon High School in San Mateo who, somehow, was supremely confident that he was destined to become a professional athlete.

From kindergarten to tenth grade all I really did was play sports, think about sports, dream about sports. I learned how to read by devouring minibios of jock stars. I learned math by computing players' averages (and my own). When I was twelve I ran the fifty-yard-dash in six seconds, which caused kids from all over the city to come to my school and race me. During a five-on-five weave drill at a summer basketball camp, the director of the camp, a recently retired professional basketball player, got called over to watch how accurately I could throw passes behind my back; he said he could have used a point guard like me when he was playing, and he bumped me up out of my grade level. I remember once hitting a home run in the bottom of the twelfth inning to win a Little League all-star game and then coming home to lie down in my uniform in the hammock in our backyard, drink lemonade, eat sugar cookies, and measure my accomplishments against the fellows featured in the just-arrived issue of *Sports Illustrated*. Christ, I remember thinking, how could life possibly get any better than this?

In junior high I would frequently take the bus crosstown, toss my backpack under my father's desk, and spend the rest of the

afternoon playing basketball with black kids. I played in all seasons and instead of all other sports. In seventh grade I developed
a double-pump jump shot, which in seventh grade was almost
unheard of. Rather than shooting on the way up, I tucked my
knees, hung in the air a second, pinwheeled the ball, then shot on
the way down. My white friends hated my new move. It seemed
tough, mannered, teenage, vaguely Negro. The more I shot like
this, the more my white friends disliked me, and the more they
disliked me, the more I shot like this. At the year-end assembly, I
was named "best athlete," and my mother said that when I went
up to accept the trophy, I even walked like a jock. At the time, I
took this as the ultimate accolade, though I realize now she
meant it as gentle mockery.

My father didn't particularly mind my mindlessness, since, in
addition to being director of the poverty program, he was also a
lifelong athlete (runner, swimmer, trophy-winning tennis player)
and sporadic sportswriter who, even now, at 94, still writes an
occasional sports column for his local suburban California weekly.
My mother, on the other hand, disapproved. Once, she said to me,
"Sometimes when people ask me if all you ever do is play sports, I
want to tell them, 'At least he's devoted to something. At least he
has an activity at which he excels,' but other times I wish you were
obsessed with something a little more permanent."

"Yes, I know," I whispered; it was very late on some Sunday
night.

"Sometimes I just want to tell those people: 'Leave me alone.
Leave him alone. He's like a dancer on that damn playfield or
ballyard or what have you.' But what I usually tell them, what I
really feel, and what I guess I'm trying to tell you now, is that I

wish you'd dedicate yourself with the same passion to a somewhat more elevated calling."

"Yes, I know," I whispered again, turning and trotting off to sleep.

SPORTS AND POLITICS have always been, for me, in curiously close conversation, alliance, overlap, competition. None of the kids I played sports with were Jewish. They called me Buddha Boy (I never quite understood this moniker—Judaism was as unfathomable to them as Buddhism?) and Ignatz (my body was small and my ears were large), asked me why anyone would want to be Jewish. When Sandy Koufax refused to pitch during the World Series, I suddenly felt proud to stay home on Yom Kippur. My father derives his identity at least as much from Hank Greenberg and Jewish boxers of the 1930s as he does from his P.S. 149 schoolmates Danny Kaye and Phil Silvers.

In high school I was athletic and thus, to a certain extent, popular. However, I worked unduly hard at it, at sports, with very little *sprezzatura,* which made me extremely unpopular among the really popular, really athletic people. Why? Because I made popularity or grace look like something less than a pure gift. Only the really popular, really athletic people knew I was unpopular, so I could, for instance, be elected, if I remember correctly, vice president of the sophomore class and yet be, in a sense, underappreciated.

Cosell knew the feeling, amplified. "I remember going to school in the morning," Cosell said in his *Playboy* interview. "A Jewish boy. I remember having to climb a back fence and run because the kids from St. Theresa's parish were after me. My drive, in a sense, relates to being Jewish and living in an age of Hitler. I think these things create insecurities in you that live forever." As if in proof of these insecurities, he said, "I am the most hated man on the face of the earth."

Still, he did have a point. He was voted the "most disliked sportscaster of the 1970s." One sign at a stadium said "Will Rogers Never Met Howard Cosell." Another sign said "Howard Is a Hemorrhoid." A contest was held: the winner got to throw a brick through a TV set while Cosell was talking on it. Buddy Hackett told Johnny Carson, "There are two schools of thought about Howard Cosell. Some people hate him like poison, and some people just hate him regular."

One Saturday morning, two medics carrying a stretcher stormed my family's front door, looking for someone who had supposedly fallen on the front steps. Later that afternoon, a middle-aged man, slightly retarded, tried to deliver a pepperoni pizza. A cop came to investigate a purported robbery. Another ambulance. A florist. An undertaker from central casting. Vehicles from most areas of the service sector were, at one point, parked virtually around the block. I was certain (though I could never prove) that my popular, athletic friends, who always gathered together to watch the proceedings with binoculars in one of their houses at the top of the hill, had orchestrated this extravaganza. Every Halloween I cowered in my basement bedroom with the doors locked, lights out, shades down, and listened to the sound of eggs hitting my house.

I had company. "Cosell, the Mouth, why don't you drop dead? There's a bomb in Rich Stadium. It will blow you up at 10 p.m., Monday." "If he comes to Green Bay on October first, I'm going to kill him, and your sheriff's department can't stop me."

"You will die now, because your government lies. I will be out in October and will be there to get you and all ABC government cheaters." The death threats always came from smaller, less cosmopolitan towns or cities—Buffalo; Green Bay; Milwaukee; Denver; Deer Lodge, Montana—to residents of which Cosell must have seemed like Sissified Civilization itself.

Every plot needs a villain, as Bill Cosby told Cosell. Cosell says that when he, Gifford, and Meredith were struggling through the first rehearsal for *MNF*, he reassured Meredith: "The Yankee lawyer and the Texas cornpone, putting each other on. You'll wear the white hat, I'll wear the black hat, and you'll have no problems from the beginning. You're going to come out of this a hero. I know this country. There's nothing this country loves more than a cowboy, especially when he's standing next to a Jew. Middle America will love you. Southern America will love you. And there are at least forty sportswriters in the country who can't wait to get at me. You'll benefit thereby. Don't worry about me, though. Because in the long run it will work for the old coach, too." Which it did, at least for a while, for longer than anyone thought possible.

Gifford was the fair-haired Hall-of-Famer. "People always looked for things in me they'd like to see in themselves," Gifford claimed. "I've never known what to think of it." Ah, but he did. "Look at him standing there, girls," Cosell liked to say within earshot of Gifford at meet-and-greets before *MNF* games. "A veritable Greek god. America's most famous football hero. The dream of the American working girl. The single most sexually dynamic man in the chronicle of the male sex." Cosell was up for this jocularity; so, in a way, was Gifford (in his memoir *The Whole Ten Yards*, he gleefully quotes his then wife Kathie Lee calling him a "love machine").

"Anyone who looked like Ichabod Crane and spoke with a nasal Brooklyn accent didn't exactly fit the sportscaster mold," Gifford said later about Cosell, in retaliation. "On top of that, Howard was Jewish."

"Of course there are critics," Cosell sighed one night on *MNF*. "There will always be critics. 'The dogs bark, but the caravan rolls on.'"

Meredith—good ole boy with a slight sideways wit—said, "Woof."

Another time, a receiver muffed an easy catch, and Meredith said, "Hey, he should be on *Saturday Night Live with Howard Cosell*," which had tanked after twelve shows. Cosell glowered.

Gifford, Meredith, and Cosell couldn't find anywhere to eat after one game, so the limo pulled into a McDonald's in a slum. Meredith urged Cosell to exit: "Ha'hrd, they want you. It's your constituency. You know, the poor, the downtrodden. You're always talking about them. Shit, Ha'hrd, here they are!"

When the Giants were playing the Cowboys on *MNF*, Cosell said, teasingly, that he wasn't impressed by the play of Meredith's and Gifford's (former) respective teams, and Meredith replied, "At least we have respective teams."

Cosell should have laughed, but he didn't. I should have laughed when my faux-friends made fun of me, but I didn't, I couldn't (and so they made more fun of me). Cosell was/I was everything they weren't: Jewish, verbal, performative, engagé, contrarian, pretentious but insecure, despising (adoring) athletics and athletes.

Instead, Cosell would tattle to *MNF* executive producer Roone Arledge: "They're doing it again. The two jocks are out to get me. They're after me again."

Instead, Cosell said to Meredith, "Don't start it, because you don't stand a chance. Get into a duel of words with me, and I'll put you away."

Instead, he said about Gifford, "He admired my command of the language, my ability to communicate, and he was shrewd enough not to engage me in a debate. He had to know he couldn't win."

Witness the adulation of words. For Cosell, language was everything, as All-American Heroism was/is for Gifford (this all blew away in a storm when Gifford's marriage and career came undone; we're in Cheever country—the perfect Connecticut home is no bulwark against the crooked timber of humanity) and Texan joie de vivre was/is for Meredith (this, too, was a crock; Meredith came to despise the "Dandy Don" mask that was his meal ticket). Once, on the air, Meredith kissed Cosell on the cheek, pretending to gag on Cosell's toupee. Cosell immediately responded by saying, "I didn't know you . . . cared." The way he paused before saying the word "cared," and the pressure that he put on the word, thrilled me to the bottom of my 15-year-old toes. "You're being extremely . . . truculent," he admonished Muhammad Ali once, and, again, what I loved was the way Cosell paused before "truculent" and the extraordinary torque he put on the word so that he seemed to be simultaneously brandishing the word as a weapon and mocking his own sesquipedalianism. In *The Whole Ten Yards,* Gifford—surely leaning more than a little on his co-writer, *Newsweek* television writer Harry Waters—says about Cosell: "His genius lay in turning his liabilities into assets. He gave his voice"—thick New Yawk honk, full of Brooklyn bile—"a dramatic, staccato delivery that grabbed you by the ears." I, too, wanted to turn my liabilities into strengths. I knew what my liabilities were; only, what were my strengths?

I HAD BEEN AWARE since I was 6 or 7 that I stuttered, but the problem would come and go; it never seemed that serious or significant. I'd successfully hid out from it, or it from me. Now, as a sophomore in high school, with my hormones trembling, my lips were, too. In class, I'd sit in back, pretending not to hear when called upon and, when pressed to respond, would produce an answer that I knew was incorrect but was the only word I could say. I devotedly studied the dictionary and thesaurus in the hope I could possess a vocabulary of such immense range that for every word, I'd know half a dozen synonyms and thus would always be able to substitute an easy word for an unspeakable one. My sentences became so saturated with approximate verbal equivalents that what I thought often bore almost no relation to what I actually said.

One day I was asked whether the origin of the American Revolution was essentially economic or philosophical. I wanted to say, as my mother and father had taught me, that revolution arises from an unfair distribution of wealth, but instead I replied: "The Whigs had a multiplicity of fomentations, ultimate or at least penultimate of which would have to be their predilection to be utterly discrete from colonial intervention, especially on numismatical pabulae." The teacher looked down at his desk. The class roared. By the end of the week, I'd been scheduled to meet with the school's speech therapist.

Miss Acker was very pretty but not especially my type: a little too cherubic to be truly inspiring. She knew I was a basketball player and proved to be surprisingly knowledgeable about the game, so for the first half hour we talked about how it doesn't matter if a guard is short if he knows how to protect the ball; what a shame it was that the high school had no girls' basketball team; how *A Sense of Where You Are* was good but *The Last Loud Roar* was probably even better.

Then she had to turn on the tape recorder, hand me a mimeographed memorandum, and say, "You've been speaking really well, Dave—only a few minor disfluencies here and there. Let me hear you read for a while."

"Oh, I read fine," I said and wasn't being intentionally insincere. I saw myself as a relatively articulate reader.

"That's funny," she said and started rummaging around in her drawer for something or other. "Almost all stutterers have at least a little trouble when it comes to oral reading."

I, on the other hand, disliked the label. It sounded like *atheist* or *heretic* or *cat burglar.*

"I don't see myself exactly as a stutterer," I said. "It's more just a case of getting nervous in certain situations. When I feel comfortable, I never have any trouble talking."

This wasn't true, but I felt pressed.

"Well, you feel comfortable with me, I hope. Why don't you read aloud that memo? We'll record it, play it back, and you tell me what you think."

At the time, my particular plague spot happened to be words beginning with vowels. This text, for one reason or another, was riddled with them. I kept opening my mouth and uttering air bubbles, half-human pops of empty repetition. Miss Acker didn't have to play the tape back for me to know it had been the very embodiment of babble, but she did, and then, raising her right eyebrow, asked, "Well?"

I explained that the whirring of the tape recorder and her ostentatious tallying of my errata had made me nervous. The proof that I wasn't just one more stutterer was that I could whisper.

"But, Dave," she said, "that's characteristic of stutterers."

"That's not true," I said. "You're lying. I know you are. You're just saying that. Stutterers cannot whisper. I know they can't."

"Yes, they can," she said. "Virtually all stutterers can whisper. You're a stutterer. I want you to admit that fact. It's an important step. Once you acknowledge it, we can get to work on correcting it. When you're a professional basketball player, I don't want to see you giving hesitant interviews at halftime."

The flattery tactic didn't work the second time, not least because she was wrong: as Howard Cosell well knew, the athletic aesthetic is always to assert that the ecstasies experienced by the body are beyond the reach of words, whereas to some cerebral people, unfortunately, the primal appeal of a warrior-athlete is nearly bottomless. I'd regularly distinguished myself from the common run of repeaters by the fact that I could whisper; now, informed that I was one among millions, I was enraged—at what or whom I didn't quite know, but enraged.

I stood and said, "I don't want your happy posters or your happy smiles or your happy basketball chitchat. I don't want to be happy. I want to be u-u-unusual." Then I did something I thought was very unusual: I tore down a poster of a seagull and ran out of the room. Having never before confronted myself and found myself in any real way wanting, I returned to her office the next day and began what still—thirty years later—feels like my life: a life limited but also defined by language.

• • •

WITHIN A WEEK, Miss Acker got me switched out of Typing into Public Speaking. The speech teacher, Mr. Roshoff, much the most charismatic teacher in the school, had been the object of my older sister's (and many other girls') crush for years. He was tall and lean and witty and brutally ironic in a way that seemed not entirely dissimilar to Cosell's manner. Every week or so, we had to present a new speech, and with those I suffered predictably, but then I hit on the idea of doing a speech imitating Cosell. This was 1972—fall, the first month of my sophomore year, the third year of *MNF*—and so I went to school on "The Mouth" the only way I could, without the aid of a VCR, which was more than a decade away. I simply watched him and thought about him as much as I could, even more than I had before.

"The Mouth" was a good nickname for him. He was such an insatiably oral guy, talking nonstop—the way my mother and sister and Mr. Roshoff did—and always pouring liquor down his throat and jamming a huge stogie in his mouth. Dick Ebersol, now president of NBC Sports, said about Cosell, "He was defined by what he said, not how he looked or spoke." As with virtually everything Dick Ebersol has ever said, this is exactly wrong. How Cosell looked and how he spoke were everything. With his pasty skin, his stoop-shouldered walk, his ridiculous toupee, his enormous ears and schnozz, he always reminded me of nothing so much as a very verbose and Jewish elephant. The sportswriter Frank Deford's paean to him nicely conveys this quality: "He is not the one with the golden locks [Gifford] or the golden tan [Meredith], but the old one, shaking, sallow, and hunched, with a chin whose purpose is not to exist as a chin but only to fade so that his face may, as the bow of a ship, break the waves and not get in the way of that voice." The things he could do with that voice: the way, every week at halftime on *MNF*, he'd extemporize the NFL highlights in that roller-coaster rhetoric of his and, in so doing, "add guts and life to a damned football game," as he said, or as Chet Forte, executive director of *MNF* for years and years, said later, "It's not a damn football game. It's a show. That's what those guys [Gifford and Meredith] never understood. They never appreciated what Howard did. He could make two 85-year-olds playing a game of marbles sound like the most exciting event in the history of sports." He'd found a way to be better than what he was reporting on, to bully reality, to make life into language.

After a week of practice, I had my Cosell imitation down. Stutterers often don't stutter when singing, whispering, or acting, and when I did my Cosell imitation, I didn't stutter. I was melodramatically grandiloquent and entertaining in the Cosellian vein. Everyone in the class loved my performance—it ended with the football purportedly landing in and thereby shutting my/Cosell's mouth—and Mr. Roshoff loved it, too. For the next three years, he rarely passed me without saying softly, out of the side of his mouth, "HEL-lo, every-BODY, this is HOW-wud Cos-SELL." It was easy to see why my sister and several of her friends had crushes on him. Still, I could imitate Howard Cosell; so what? So could and did a lot of other people. Where did that get me, exactly?

TOWARD THE END of my sophomore year—Mother's Day, actually—I went to the beach with my mother. After a while she dozed off, so I walked along the shore until I was invited to join a game of Tackle the Guy with the Ball. After I scored several times in a row, several of the other guys ganged up to tackle the guy with the ball (me), and down I went. Suddenly my left leg was tickling my right ear, the water was lapping at my legs, and a crowd of a hundred people gathered around me to speculate as to whether I was permanently paralyzed. Bursting through the throng, my mother threw up her hands and wailed at me, "See? See what sports will do to you?" She was very sympathetic later on, but her first reaction was, approximately, "I told you so."

I had a badly broken leg—my left femur—and was in traction the entire summer, but when the doctor misread the X-ray and removed the body cast too early, I had a pin inserted in my leg, and I used a leg brace and crutches my entire junior year. I still stutter slightly, but in high school my stutter was so severe that it effectively defined who I was. My whole life was structured around the idea of doing one thing so well that people forgave me for, and I forgave myself for, my "disfluency" (Miss Acker's term). With the jockocracy newly closed to me, I became, nearly overnight, an insanely overzealous chess player, carried along by the aftermath of the Fischer-Spassky World Championship. I got to the point that I dreamed in chess notation, but I was certainly never going to become a chess whiz, and I rationalized to myself that if one could be, as Bobby Fischer was, the best chess player in the world but still a monster and a moron, then the game wasn't interesting, and so I abandoned it after several months and joined the school paper.

By my senior year I'd recovered well enough from my broken leg that I was twelfth man on the varsity basketball team and second doubles in tennis, but sports no longer meant much to me. All that physical expression had gone inside; language was my new channel. I suddenly loved reading; I became the editor of the paper; my parents (especially my mother) were thrilled; it was sickening. I spent no more time on my studies than I had before, but now instead of six hours a day playing sports, it was six hours a day working on the paper, writing nearly every article, taking every photograph, attending journalism conferences around the Bay Area, submitting my work to every possible high school journalism competition, submitting the paper and my work (they were virtually synonymous) for competitions. My bible was *New Journalism,* an anthology of pieces edited by Tom Wolfe, which I read over and over again. I thought I'd become a new journalist, à la Hunter Thompson or Joan Didion.

In college, though, writing for the weekly, weakly student magazine, I got in trouble for making stuff up. Also, I was trepidatious—still—about calling people on the phone (I couldn't imitate Cosell), and so I crabwalked into creative-writing courses. I'd become a fiction writer. I'd make stuff up, and that would be okay. The only problem, as I discovered in graduate school, was that compared to other fiction writers, I'm not very interested in making stuff up. I'm much more interested in contemplating the so-called real world, including, alas, the world of sports.

I've now written several books of fiction and nonfiction, and to my astonishment and horror, half of them deal more or less explicitly with sports. My first novel concerns a sportswriter's vicarious relationship with a college basketball player. My book *Black Planet* is a fan's diary of an NBA season, with particular focus on how race is the true and taboo topic of the sport (hi, Mom and Dad!). I recently compiled a book of koanlike quotations uttered by the Japanese baseball player Ichiro Suzuki. And now here is *Body Politic.* As my daughter says, "Daddy writes about exercise."

In *The Wound and the Bow*, Edmund Wilson analyzes how various writers, such as Dickens, Wharton, and Hemingway, used the central wound of their life as the major material of their art. Throughout her entire childhood, a writer I know worked fiendishly hard in the hope of becoming a professional ballet dancer. She entered the Harkness Ballet trainee program at eighteen, but she left after less than a year. It's only right that her first book, published a couple of years ago when she was in her mid-forties, is a collection of stories set in the world of ballet and that her novel-in-progress is told from the point of view of George Balanchine. In *Rocky*, asked what he sees in dowdy Adrian, Rocky says, "She fills gaps." I was a great child athlete, and I just assumed this play-paradise would last forever. It didn't. Writing about it fills gaps.

I wish I could say instead that the material I keep returning to is seventeenth-century Flemish painting or the Cold War or unified field theory, but it's not. I keep coming back to sports, of all things. Much of what I write seems to feature an exceedingly verbal person contemplating an exceedingly physical person. I return over and over to the endlessly complex dialectic between body and mind. Whenever we talk about the body, we inevitably lie, but the body itself never lies. Our bodies always betray us—always tell us what we're really feeling (desire, fear, hatred, rapture). The body-in-motion is, for me, the site of the most meaning. At a deep spot in the river, Howard Cosell showed me the way across; he showed me where to look and, looking, how to stand.

ON THE NEED TO CONNECT
WITH SOMETHING LARGER
THAN YOURSELF

WATCH THE NBA SOMETIME ON ABC OR TNT OR ESPN; WATCH how the camera constantly cuts back and forth between the two head coaches pacing the sidelines and the ten players running up and down the court, as if to imply that the coaches are omnipotent puppeteers and the players their particularly lithe puppets. Watch NCAA basketball sometime on ESPN; listen to Dick Vitale refer over and over again to the coach as "The Orchestrator." Thus does race myth get reified: maybe black men can walk on the moon, but white men still man Mission Control. (Paging Muhammad Ali/Howard Cosell . . .)

Eighty percent of NBA players are African-American, and two-thirds of those 80 percent grew up without a father. One of the principal reasons that current Los Angeles Lakers and former

Chicago Bulls coach Phil Jackson has been so successful is his ability to function as a subtly paternal rather than sadistically paternalistic leader of a group of young black men who might have use for a mentor but not a tyrant. In Chicago, Jackson coached the Bulls to six championships. In Los Angeles, he's transformed the Lakers, who the previous three years had failed to fuse the talents of all-star center Shaquille O'Neal and all-star guard Kobe Bryant into anything resembling cohesion, into a team that won the NBA championship three consecutive years (2000–2002). In the words of former Lakers forward/center John Salley, who rarely played in games but who appeared to function as a sort of *ex cathedra* assistant coach and team spokesman, "With Phil, it's 'You're a man. I'm a man. I'm going to help you be a better man.'" Players seem stunned and grateful that Jackson neither panders to their wishes nor preys on their insecurities.

Most of the coaches in the NBA are naggers; players call such coaches "little bitches," according to Charley Rosen, a novelist who wrote a book, *More Than a Game,* with Jackson about their basketball-based friendship. Black players, especially, get tired of, especially, white coaches yipping at them. Players complain that most coaches don't speak to them "man-to-man"; most coaches can't fathom how their tirades can carry racial connotations to players. The P. J. Carlesimo–Latrell Sprewell incident of several years ago is the benchmark example of this. I think also of the clenches between Boston's former coach Rick Pitino and star Antoine Walker; Philadelphia's former coach Larry Brown and Sixers point guard Allen Iverson; New York's former coach Jeff Van Gundy and Sprewell. Jackson seems to grasp that in the white-managed, black-content-provider NBA, the dialectic between coaches and players must rise above the punitive patriarchy of the 350-year-old American Race War; the conversation has to find a new groove.

DURING THE PLAYER introductions before a late February 2000 game between the Portland TrailBlazers and the Lakers, the Portland cheerleaders set an enormous bonfire aflame, quite close to the Lakers' bench. The Rose Garden was absolutely collegiate in its cacophonous Blazermania—raucous, riotous, tribal. While pretending to diagram a play for O'Neal, Jackson made an almost comically explicit point of standing as close to the fire as he could without burning himself. In the sense-annihilating din of fan frenzy, Shaq couldn't possibly have heard a word Jackson was saying or, in the flashing lights, decoded a single symbol of what Jackson was supposedly diagramming. What was he up to?

Halfway through the first quarter, Jackson called time-out immediately after Los Angeles had inbounded the ball with Portland leading 8–6. Before the teams met, he'd said this was his "most important regular-season game in thirty-three years in the NBA," which, coming from such an exponent of understatement and indirection, seemed improbable hyperbole, but the game did involve two teams with identical records—45–11, the best in the league—and both possessing eleven-game win streaks. Los Angeles had lost the last seven games in Portland. It still seemed a rather abrupt and alarming time-out.

Lakers guard Brian Shaw, who had inbounded the ball, said, "We were just bringing the ball in and he called a time-out. Everybody looked at him and was surprised. I thought, 'Uh-oh. He must have called something in the huddle and we didn't run it the right way.' We all went over there, thinking we must have done something. So I said, 'Did we do something?' And he said, 'No. I'm just messing around.' We just went over and had some water and sat down. And then he said, 'Okay. Get ready to go.'"

Jackson's brinkmanship reminded his players that it's finally just a game they're playing and that they, too, are supposed to be messing around having fun (on the Lakers' first possession of the game, guard Ron Harper had shot an air ball). Jackson also communicated, to his team as well as to Portland, that the Lakers were unfazed, that amidst all this primitivism, they were maintaining their poise; unmistakably, too, that he was in control—not only of the team, of course, but of the building. *We're running the show, not them.* When the Lakers returned to the court, Shaw scored on a driving layup.

PRETENDING TO praise Pat Riley before Los Angeles faced Miami in March 2000, Jackson said, "I have great admiration for his attention to detail, the driving, authoritarian kind of dictatorship that he runs his teams with. And the motivational work that he does—it keeps people very busy and very driven." Jackson uses instead what he calls the I Know That You Know That I Know method of coaching. "What are you looking at me for? You know what you did wrong," he'll say when a player looks to the sideline after a miscue. "I'm no savior," he said when he arrived in Los Angeles in the summer of 1999. "They have to be the savior of themselves."

Off the court, though, Jackson seems to want to be their savior and doesn't seem to hear how high-handed he can seem. He's one of the most relentless referee baiters in the NBA. He referred to Orlando as a "plastic city"—not exactly a groundbreaking position—and given the opportunity to apologize, refused. His first season in Los Angeles, he repeatedly called Portland "the best team money can buy"—sour grapes over the fact that he couldn't convince the Lakers management to spend the money for Scottie Pippen. Asked, before the Portland game, about the purpose of recently introducing a psychologist to the team, he said, "What we're building or trying to build is a good community—trying to teach players how to be inclusive and how to do things that are not always male-oriented. You want to be independent? Want to be your own man?" He said "man" in a light, gentle, but still surprising parody of black dialect. "We're teaching them how to be not dependent or codependent but interdependent, so you're relying on each other but you're still having your own space." At the beginning of the 1999–2000 season, he said, "The Lakers are all autistic in some form or fashion. I don't mean to say that as a snide remark towards a certain population in our society. But they"—the Lakers—"have a limitation of their attention span. A lot of it is probably due to too much rap music going in their ears or coming out of their being. So they need to get a focal point that lasts longer than a TV commercial." Kobe Bryant, who spent a large portion of his childhood in Italy, said he found Jackson's giving him *The White Boy Shuffle,* a novel about a black child raised in a privileged white community, presumptuous. Giving Shaq a copy of Nietzsche's *Ecce Homo*—doesn't this smack of noblesse oblige?

On the other hand, Jackson almost never calls plays, which he believes makes players feel as if they're on a string—his. This hands-off impulse comes from his practice of Zen Buddhism, with its strong emphasis on egolessness, but also from his innate temperament, which he once described as "low-key, not comatose but close to it." His ex-wife, June, when she was still married to Jackson, said, "It's comfortable to be with him. He's quiet inside." And it's so loud over there in all those other huddles. When I bumped into him in the elevator at the Benson Hotel in Portland, he had the least hegemonic presence of any coach of any sport at any level I've ever encountered. Whenever Bryant goes one-on-one, Jackson will typically remove him from the game and then rarely say anything, trusting that the message will get through, though delivered obliquely. "He's not in-your-face," says Bryant. "He's subtle." Asked what distinguished Jackson from other coaches they'd played for, more than one Laker said, "During the game, he *sits down*." Players thrill to this un–Bobby Knight–ness.

The son of two Pentecostal ministers; role player on the championship New York Knicks teams of the 1970s coached by Red Holzman, who preached team basketball; idealist whose social values were formed in the '60s; lifelong student of Zen and admirer of the Lakota Sioux, Jackson was destined to be the anti-coach coach. Many years ago, after watching the Bulls play the Nuggets in Denver, Jackson's sister-in-law told him that, watching him coach, she "started crying because I realized this is exactly what you were meant to do. You're so comfortable out there. It just seems so right."

When Jackson was four, his mother hung a sign over his bed with a quotation from John 3:16—so popular now on fundamentalist fans' placards at sporting events: "For God so loved the world, that he gave his only begotten Son, that whosoever believeth in him should not perish, but have everlasting life." Jackson's mother was a stern authoritarian; his father was a do-gooder. Jackson has contrived a way to combine the personalities of his parents by becoming a Wizard of Oz who insists on stepping out from behind the curtain to let the whole group play with the control switches, an authority figure whose authority derives from his (strategic) willingness to deconstruct that authority.

THE DAY AFTER the Portland game, the Lakers played the lowly Vancouver (now Memphis) Grizzlies in Los Angeles, and "lethargy" doesn't begin to describe the absence of energy in Staples Center that evening. As Jackson would say afterward, "We were somnambulant out there. We were the walking wounded in their sleep." Most coaches would have been calling time-outs, hollering at players, madly making substitutions. Perversely, Jackson did very nearly nothing for the entire game. He sat passively on the bench, a mirror reflecting back to the players their own quiescence, daring them to find a way out of their morass themselves. He even let O'Neal stay on the floor after picking up his fourth foul midway through the fourth quarter; Shaq picked up his fifth shortly thereafter, and Jackson removed him with the game tied. Immediately after O'Neal went to the bench, the Lakers hit three consecutive 3-pointers, and the Grizzlies never truly threatened the rest of the way.

"That's natural, a letdown after last night," Jackson said afterward. "You have to measure it out and find a way to win. It's good for them to adjust to that. I think they're really learning and growing."

June Jackson once said, "Sometimes he keeps things moving by not doing anything. With Phil, there's a flowing rather than a forcing."

Jackson's most famous flowing-rather-than-forcing occurred when Chicago's Scottie Pippen refused to enter a 1994 playoff game with 1.8 seconds left against New York. Jackson walked into the Bulls' locker room and said, "What happened has hurt us. Now you have to work this out. You've got two minutes to get together, to talk softly between yourselves."

Nearly every other NBA coach would have used the occasion as an opportunity to solidify his own power base; instead of doing that, Jackson, in his own words, "stepped back and let the team come up with its own solution." In the locker room, Bill Cartwright made an unusually emotional appeal to his team-mates; the incident reportedly brought the team closer together. Jackson's goal is to yield control at a superficial level in order to regain it at a more profound level by creating an environment in which the "players become policemen of themselves, and that's really more fun for a coach to watch than anything else."

THE ONE MOMENT during the entire Vancouver game when Bryant seemed to me at all happy was when he zigzagged through the defense for a thrilling reverse dunk, and when I asked him if this was so, he smiled and laughed.

"Some of the things Phil does I find hilarious," Bryant said.

"Intentionally hilarious or accidentally hilarious?"

"Like whenever I'm doing something and he goes 'No, no, no.'"

With four minutes remaining in the third quarter of the Port-land game, Bryant lost the ball when, as he's wont to do, he tried to go one-on-one—a serious violation in the Triangle Offense, which Jackson believes in so strongly because it "empowers every-body on the team by making them more involved in the offense, and demands that they put their individual needs second to those of the group." Jackson immediately removed Bryant, and the two of them had an unusually animated discussion on the sideline. Asked what they'd discussed while he was on the bench, Bryant skirted the question somewhat by saying, "The building was so loud you couldn't hear each other, so we had to shout. We had a system breakdown out there and so I took the ball to the hoop. He wanted to know what had happened and I explained it to him. He just wanted us to regroup."

Jackson put Bryant back in the game before even a minute of game-time had elapsed. He wound up scoring 22 points and committing only one more turnover the rest of the evening. Neither "controloholic" (Jackson's word) nor helplessly, hopelessly laissez-faire, Jackson is firm but open to persuasion. "Part of life," as Jackson says, "is getting sucked into something with others."

Against Portland, O'Neal made 9 of 13 free throws—slightly lower than the league average but for O'Neal a sterling performance. After the game, Jackson said, "The reason we won the game is Shaq converted his free throws. That's the story of the game." Before the season started, Jackson took O'Neal to task immediately and publicly by telling a reporter from *Sports Illustrated* that if O'Neal continued to be unable to make free throws late in games, he'd be unable to be the leader of the team. The reporter even asked Jackson if he'd told O'Neal this yet; Jackson said no.

Mark Schwarz, a Los Angeles–based correspondent for ESPN, said, "I asked Jackson, 'Didn't you find that to be a risky move?' And he said, 'Well, not really. If you have an elephant in your living room, you can choose to ignore it, but sooner or later it's going to have to be dealt with.'" Confronting the issue directly but indirectly—a signature Jackson maneuver—he challenged O'Neal, who paid far more attention to that aspect of his game during the '99–'00 season than he ever had before, albeit with no impact on his final percentage. (He did improve to 56 percent in '01–'02 and 62 percent in '02–'03.)

By all accounts, considerable tension had developed between O'Neal and Bryant during the three years before Jackson came to Los Angeles. Although Bryant is younger and less proven, O'Neal reportedly needs the validation of others more, has a more fragile ego, is more insecure. Bryant knows how great he is and dares anyone to tell him differently. Knowing this about the two of them, Jackson and the Lakers' management opted to celebrate O'Neal whenever possible, to anoint him Alpha, even at the risk of denying this status to Bryant. Jerry West, the Lakers' then general manager, said, "When teams prepare for us, the person they prepare for is Shaquille O'Neal. He's the Man. Kobe Bryant is just a young guy with a world of talent." Jackson has gone so far as to compare O'Neal favorably to both Wilt Chamberlain and Kareem Abdul-Jabbar. Jackson realized that Bryant has many of the same gifts that Jordan has, but that he doesn't yet have the same court sense or leadership ability; he never played college basketball, and he's still only twenty-five. Rather than allow Bryant's freelancing impulse to go unfettered, Jackson repeatedly reins him in. Because of the equity Jackson built with six championships before coming to the Lakers, and now three more with the Lakers, he has (just barely) the license to take such liberties, even with players of Bryant's caliber.

HOW MUCH OF Jackson's fabled self-confidence is a by-product of his happy fate to coach the two most dominant players in the league, first Michael Jordan and now Shaquille O'Neal? As Bryant said at the beginning of Jackson's first year in L.A., "An aura? No. He's got six rings. That's a pretty good thing to have with you." Jackson maintains a chilly margin of mystery around himself partly, I think, as a quite consciously crafted technique to get his players to stay tuned through the grind of an 82-game season. By being interestingly paradoxical—gentle but not warm, relaxed yet in charge—he doesn't bore the team to death; he keeps people alertly off guard. (For instance, he agreed to be interviewed only via e-mail.) He's a freaky control freak who sees and seizes the benefits of granting to his charges a semifreedom. Jackson's friend Charley Rosen describes him as a "benevolent dictator."

When I asked Jackson if he saw any connection between his apparently emancipated coaching style and the racial demographics of the NBA, he characteristically slipped the noose of any too-tight definition by saying, "I don't think black or white make a difference to coaches. I think control is the issue. If I'm responsible for this team, I'll be damned if I let some kids take me down. It's my job attitude."

Jackson's blessing and his curse—what makes him both a winning coach and a rather enigmatic person (his effectiveness and inscrutability are closely related)—is his extraordinary detachment. In the summer of 2003, when sexual assault charges were filed against Bryant, Jackson's terse response was: "As his coach and mentor, he has my full support." June Jackson would get frustrated by how little emotion Phil displayed after big victories. She once suggested that he wave to her in the stands after games to let her know how happy he was about winning. He took the suggestion under advisement. She also theorized that his passivity is a survival technique he adopted in response to the speaking-in-tongues fanaticism of his childhood home.

"Sometimes I wish we could play in a gym without any people [in the stands]," Jackson once said, "and try to play the perfect game where you don't make any mistakes and maybe if there's a mistake it's of omission, not commission, and everything is done at the right moment, at the right time, and each decision is the right one and everyone can ride that decision-making wave." In an e-mail, I asked him, "Many players seem to view their role as being not only to compete but to entertain; is there anything you like about the performance aspects of being a coach?" His only response was: "The performance aspect of basketball enhances some players' ability and hinders others'." If Buddhism, a fundamentalist childhood, and political idealism are the building blocks of his leadership style, they're also the ingredients of his spookily hyper-rational perfectionism.

Asked what his own weaknesses were, Jackson cited having too high expectations and not offering praise often enough: pure PK—preacher's kid. "The greatness of Michael Jordan is his competitive drive. The weakness of Michael Jordan is his competitive drive," Jackson once said. "My weakness is also competitiveness to excess." June refused to play board games with him. Every year during the playoffs, he throws a barrage of verbal brickbats at opposing players, coaches, and fans; Jackson sees this as crucial psychological warfare, but its main effect is to make him seem petty.

The day before an April 2000 game in Los Angeles between the Lakers and the San Antonio Spurs—what was billed (accurately, it turned out) as a likely preview of the 2000 Western Conference finals—Jackson said, "This is a team we know we not only want to beat, we want to beat soundly. We want to let them know that it's going to be very difficult to play us in the playoffs;

that whatever they consider February first was, it was an illusion." In February, in the Alamodome, the Spurs beat the Lakers by 24 points—Los Angeles's worst defeat of the year. Jackson went on to say about San Antonio, "They showed their moxie last year in an abbreviated season, winning the asterisk season. But you don't know what a team has until they've played an 82-game season and you come out in the end."

After the anticlimactic game—which the Spurs won easily when Shaq sat out with a sprained ankle, rendering the game meaningless as a gauge of how the teams match up against each other—San Antonio coach Gregg Popovich said about Jackson's disparaging remarks, "He's a great coach who's won a lot of championships. It's just hard to figure what his motivation would be for comments he's made. I'm chalking it up to being childish."

Luckily for Jackson, and for the Lakers, whatever tendency he might have toward petulance is balanced by his instinct for playfulness. At the Lakers' first team meeting Jackson's first year, they practiced without a ball. Other practices have been conducted in complete silence. What other NBA coach would have been unable to keep a smile off his face when his player (the Bulls' Dennis Rodman, in 1996) head-butted a self-serious referee (Ted Bernhardt)? "Don't you think it's interesting having Dennis around?" Jackson asked. On the way to a practice during the 1994 playoff series against the Knicks, Jackson redirected the team bus to the Battery for an impromptu group tour of the Statue of Liberty. During a midseason slump, he advised the Bulls to order up some pizza and beer to their hotel room and just relax. Lakers guard Derek Fisher, who read about the pizza-and-beer remedy in Jackson's 1995 book, *Sacred Hoops,* says, "That struck me as odd that a coach would recommend you go out and have a couple of drinks and relax and be yourself for a change, and not worry so much about trying to be who somebody else wants you to be. That's him. He sees where a team can be. And he sees the steps in between, getting there."

"He's absolutely unpredictable," says Rosen, who was Jackson's assistant coach for three years when he coached the Albany Patroons in the CBA. "Players never know what to expect, and it keeps things interesting. 'What is this guy gonna do next?' Our first year in Albany, the team was in the doldrums. One day somebody goes out to the Albany airport to pick up Lewis Brown, who had just flown in from California. He comes in, suits up for practice, and goes out onto the court. The guys on the team realize, hey, this team might be broken up; there's going to be a change here, which in those days was a big deal. Everybody on the team basically took turns battering this poor guy. Every time he turned around, somebody was hitting him. After practice, Brown took a shower and was sent back to California. Phil brought this guy in, didn't say a word, no introductions, no threats, nothing. It was a test for these guys whether they were going to stick up for each other, and it worked. Everybody banded together. The team suddenly started playing aggressively and won eight or nine games in a row, and we won the championship that year."

WITH TWENTY-FOUR seconds remaining in the game and the Lakers leading by three, Portland called time-out. Jackson spent much of the time-out talking to Brian Shaw. "Questions were coming up on how we were going to defend certain plays," Shaw said. "I was just going over and giving him our perspective from the bench: 'This is what they're doing. We feel more comfortable doing it like this.' I play that role all the time. He said to us from the beginning of the year, 'You guys are out on the floor. You have a feel for what's going on. Don't be afraid to come to me and tell me what you see.'"

By contrast, Mike Dunleavy, the Portland coach, ran onto the court at the end of the time-out, yelling last-second instructions to Greg Anthony, who turned his back on him and walked away.

The Lakers prevented the Blazers from executing the play they wanted to run. With eight seconds left, Scottie Pippen was forced to toss up a jumper from twenty-five feet away; the ball bounced off the rim into the corner. Portland's Steve Smith caught the ball and, panicking a bit, threw up a desperation shot with five seconds still left on the clock. The Lakers rebounded, and the game was over. According to Jackson, the Lakers read the play perfectly, "made the switches correctly, and chased them into the spaces they couldn't operate from." He credited his players, in particular guard Ron Harper, "who saw and read what was coming up." It was a duel between two very good bands. The Lakers were the tighter band. They won.

Asked once what the best part of basketball is, Jackson said it was the ride back to the airport after winning a game on an opponent's floor. I e-mailed him to ask why he particularly savored the road victory; he replied, "Winning on the road represents the ability to overcome great odds and to perform inside a hostile environment. It's delicious!"

When Jackson says, "The most effective way to forge a winning team is to call on the players' need to connect with something larger than themselves," I want to retain my skepticism. I know how bottomless the selfishness of human nature is, how fragile the bonds of any (especially artificially constructed) community are, how calculated and in some ways contradictory Jackson's persona is. There's a certain *Stepford Wives* quality to the unanimity of players' encomia about Jackson, a certain aspect of black athletes returning to white reporters, in an endless feedback loop, the same media clichés they printed last week: "Phil's at peace with himself; that's what he's trying to bring to us, that peace and that harmony and that resolve that he has within himself," etc.

And yet when I asked Harper, who played for Jackson in Chicago for several years before he joined him in Los Angeles in '99, if I could talk to him for a few minutes about Jackson, he said, "Fuck Phil Jackson, that sorry son of a bitch." If a player had said this about nearly any other coach in the NBA, it would have been difficult to take as anything besides straightforward venom. However, in this locker room (in which Shaquille O'Neal was teaching the *Los Angeles Times* beat reporter how to dance), with this team (which in a certain sense was still only mimicking secondhand notions about coming together, but in so doing was taking the first steps toward actually coming together, in the same way that saying "I love you" is the first step toward falling in love), from this player (whose reputation had always been that of a one-dimensional shooter until joining up with Jackson in Chicago, where he became a defensive specialist and floor leader), about this coach (who on media day in Los Angeles made certain that the first people the press met were the rookies, followed by

role players, then the starters, then the stars, then lastly himself—
yielding the stage to his players or underlining that he's in charge,
or both?; that's the question he's so good at lodging in players'
minds, that's the ace of his magical coaching trick), it was, I
think, a joke and, as such, pure praise.

FAIRY TALE OF REINVENTION
AND ESCAPE

The Seattle SuperSonics, in their second home game of the 2001–2002 season, were losing to the Utah Jazz. The crowd, less than two-thirds of capacity, was losing focus. With a few minutes left in the first half, the Sonics were down by 9, but they went on a brief run. A Sonics player blocked a shot. Howard Schultz, 47, the chairman and chief global strategist of Starbucks and the new principal owner of the Sonics, and his 15-year-old son, Jordan, jumped out of their front-row, center-court seats, yelling, pointing at the Jazz player who got his shot blocked, really getting in his face. "I'm a fan at heart," Schultz has said. "I still see the world and the games through the eyes of a fan. I want everyone to know that. I used to be one of those fans who sat way up in the second tier. I know what that's like and I won't forget."

Schultz is a nostalgist who is forever measuring the present against the fable of his boyhood.

The Sonics came out flat for the second half. Trailing by 10 to 15 points all game, they rallied again in the fourth quarter, but a crucial call went against Seattle: offensive goaltending (clearly, the correct call). As the ref ran back down the court, Schultz jumped to his feet, waved his arms, hollered at her.

Schultz, who is 6'2", played a game of one-on-one with Jordan, who is 6'4" and weighs 190 pounds and was winning the game. "So," Schultz says, "I decided I had to play dirty." After a few plays, Jordan grabbed the ball and said, "Dad, if you don't stop that, I'm going to have to kick your ass." Schultz broke his nose going for a rebound in a pickup basketball game.

Schultz frequently emphasizes that "the Sonics are a public trust" and that his primary motivation in purchasing the team is not to feed his own ego or to make money but to "return the team to where it once was" (the Sonics won the NBA championship twenty-five years ago) by building trust within the organization and between the fans and the players, and restoring a sense of civic pride and communal spirit about the team. A few days before Christmas 2002, while I was talking to him in the lobby of the Sonics' practice facility, one of us dropped a dime on the floor. Schultz bent down to pick it up and offered it to me, since it wasn't clear which one of us had dropped it. "You think I can be bribed so easily?" I asked. Schultz blanched, and he took a full step back. In Schultz's world, money is obviously such a deep subtext that it can never be mentioned explicitly in public, even if it's only a joke, only a dime. A minute or two later, as if to recover, he stage-whispered to the Sonics' public-relations director to tell me about second-year player Desmond Mason's visiting a terminally ill teenager.

• • •

"HOWARD, DON'T do this. You're naïve. Don't aim too high," Schultz quotes his friends telling him when he was deciding whether to buy the Sonics. "But"—goes the inevitable punch line—"I want to aim high." Schultz has a tendency to phrase every major business decision as if it were a case of Icarus flying too close to the sun. Several years ago, at a social function in Los Angeles, Schultz told NBA commissioner David Stern to call him if the Sonics were ever up for sale. Schultz says, "I never expected him to give me a call and say, 'Are you ready?'" Stern contacted Schultz and told him and the owner of the Sonics at the time, Barry Ackerley, to work out the deal. The deal was finalized in November 2000; the purchase price was $200 million. Schultz, whose share of Starbucks is worth $350 million, owns 40 percent of the Basketball Club of Seattle—the Sonics and the WNBA Seattle Storm. He's chairman and one of fourteen investors, nearly all of whom are Seattle-area businessmen.

When Schultz became the owner of the Sonics, he said, "I never thought something like this would happen to someone like me. I was born on the other side of the tracks, but only in America. I'm really excited. For me and my family, this is a dream come true." Schultz grew up in the Bayview Projects in the Canarsie section of Brooklyn and was the first member of his family to graduate from college (a B.A. in business from Northern Michigan University, which he attended on a football scholarship, though a broken jaw in his freshman year ended his playing days).

After graduating from college in 1975, Schultz worked in marketing for Xerox and then as vice president of Hammarplast, USA, a division of a Swedish housewares company. In 1981, he

made a business call on a tiny coffee-bean store in Pike Place
Market in Seattle, was handed a mug with freshly brewed coffee,
"took a small, tentative sip, and my eyes shot wide open. I felt as
though I had discovered a whole new continent." Schultz is
deeply drawn to the mythology of brief transcendence, the
mini-frisson, the ersatz escape, the tempest in a coffee cup or on
a court.

After a year of lobbying Starbucks, he was hired as director of
retail operations and marketing. In 1983, on a business trip to
Italy, he had his Saul-on-the-road-to-Damascus epiphany: "Starbucks had missed the point—completely missed it. *This is so
powerful!* I thought. *This is the link.* The connection to the people
who loved coffee did not have to take place only in their homes,
where they ground and brewed whole-bean coffee. What we had
to do was unlock the romance and mystery of coffee firsthand, in
coffee bars. The Italians understood the personal relationship that
people could have to coffee, its social aspect. I couldn't believe
that Starbucks was in the coffee business, yet was overlooking so
central an element of it." Once, long ago, in the old country, they
got it right.

Starbucks reluctantly agreed to give Schultz an espresso kiosk
in the back of one of its four stores, and although it was "over-
whelmingly successful," Schultz was unable to persuade Starbucks to transform itself from a coffee-roasting enterprise into a
chain of specialty coffee bar/bean shops. In 1985 he left Starbucks to start Il Giornale, which was based on the Italian model
and quickly expanded to three units. In 1987 he and his
investors bought Starbucks for $3.8 million; at the time, it had
11 stores and 100 employees. By 1996, Starbucks had 1,015
stores worldwide, including in Japan and Singapore. Starbucks

now averages 25 million customers a week, hires 700 new employees per month, opens 3 new stores a day, has more than 7,400 stores in thirty-seven countries on four continents, and in 2004 was called by *Fortune* magazine "possibly the most dynamic new brand to be conceived over the past two decades." "It's not about money," Schultz says. "It's about pursuing a dream." It's never about reality; it's always about the dream about reality.

WHEN I ASKED Schultz why he had bought the Sonics, he said, "First off, I have such a passionate love of this game. And my fondest memories of my relationship with my dad are based on the two of us going to Yankee Stadium and Madison Square Garden; in both cases we never sat closer than a mile away, but I have such memories of us sitting together. Because he was always working, it was the only time when we were father and son. Those memories are steeped in my relationship with sports and my relationship with my dad." Whatever this assertion's truth-value, it betrays Schultz's perfect instinct for mythmaking; almost every business gesture he makes appeals to that atavistic part of us that wants to believe in some time in the way back beyond when things were simpler, purer, better. Schultz's house is an English Manor, with different periods scattered about, as if to suggest new additions made every hundred years or so, backforming lineage.

Schultz, who had been a Sonics season-ticket holder for nearly twenty years, said, "Last year [2000–2001] I watched an implosion. I think the fans were disenfranchised from the team and the players. And the players acted as if they were just going through the motions. If I look at the fracturing of the SuperSonics over the last few years, the word 'trust' is all over this thing, because the fans lost trust in this team, the players lost trust in one another, the players lost trust in the organization, the organization lost trust in the players. When you're building trust and confidence in a product or an experience, everything you do matters. Everything. I'm acutely aware of verbal and nonverbal signs that the fan is experiencing because that is my business within Starbucks."

Upon assuming ownership of the team in spring 2002, Schultz shook fans' hands as they came in to Key Arena for the last two games of the season, and he solicited their suggestions both in person and via mail and e-mail. He held a question-and-answer session with more than a hundred season-ticket holders. He held focus groups and fan forums. He spends an hour a week calling ex–season-ticket holders, urging them to "come to a game as our guest" in the hope that they'll reconsider and re-up.

Asked how he thought his experience with Starbucks would influence his ownership of the Sonics, Schultz replied, "I know you can't superimpose the Starbucks culture on a different industry. But the similarity between Starbucks and the Sonics is this: the fan is the customer. The fan has to be able to think, 'Despite the fact that the ticket price is high, this is something that makes me feel good, and I enjoy it, and I want to keep doing it.' The fans will come first, as do Starbucks customers. We have to be fan-centric. We will put them first, and we will bring a winner back. We need to fill those seats, but not by marketing gimmicks."

A COUPLE OF DAYS before interviewing Schultz, I attended the Sonics–Minnesota Timberwolves game. Walking in to Key Arena, you hear funky jazz and classic Isley Brothers hits rather than the previously nearly exclusive dose of hip-hop; according to

Schultz, fans have to be able either to dance to the song or know the words. On Legends Drive, the jerseys of former Sonics stars Lenny Wilkins, Jack Sikma, Nate McMillan, and Fred Brown are showcased. Team photos of every previous Sonics team are framed. You can compare your wing span with Rashard Lewis's, your shoe size with Jerome James's size 22; you can compare your Pop-a-Shot score with that of Brent Barry; you can compare your hand print with those of all the Sonics. A video monitor shows the Sonics' "Back to Basics" ad campaign: a 1950s Mission Control announcer and crew-cut white players attempt to teach the old-school fundamentals of shooting, passing, and dribbling to the Sonics, who ignore the instructions and show off their own funky dunks, between-the-legs dribbles, and fancy passes. The Sonics lowered the prices on 40 percent of the upper-level seats. For ten dollars, a fan can buy a hot dog and a Coke and a nose-bleed seat. Concessions are reduced by 25 percent during "Sonics Warm-up Hour." The money fans spend at Sonics games earns points for future purchases.

Kids under 16 are allowed to sit next to the court during pregame warm-ups and take a foul shot on the court after the game. The players' jerseys and the logo on the arena floor have the green-and-gold colors and retro design of past glory days. The public-address announcer, rather than simply announcing the game, as he used to do, is now engaged in a constant, chattering conversation with the fans: "This is Desmond Mason's first appearance in the game. Let's all welcome him to the action." At halftime, former players mingle with fans and a "fan gauntlet" forms, through which the Sonics pass on the way back to the court; every night, different fans form the gauntlet. Fifteen people try to win $100 by making a shot from the free-throw line or at the top of the key. Two fans are escorted, with great to-do, from "upper bowl" seats down to pretty good but not great first-tier seats. The Sasquatch mascot is much more in the spotlight than he was before, running around the arena, holding up signs and generating noise and hugging kids. The blimp that used to fly around dropping only a few envelopes full of game tickets and coupons to local restaurants and stores now drops ten envelopes. During time-outs, young kids and/or a team of male dancers dance with the female dancers, who show less cleavage and dance less sexily than they used to; two kids, wearing Sonics players' jerseys and shoes, compete to see who can run up and down the court and shoot the ball into the hoop without stumbling; and on the video screen a kid "ace reporter" asks Coach Nate McMillan how to become a professional basketball player.

Schultz lives and dies with every play, the way a kid does. Several fans said that one thing they really like is the animation Schultz shows on the sideline during the games. "At least you can tell Howard cares" is how more than one fan put it; the previous owner, Barry Ackerley, looked and acted utterly cadaverous. When the play goes poorly, Schultz slumps back. If a Sonics player makes a showy or individualistic play, Schultz tends to be relatively undemonstrative (Brent Barry's spectacular behind-the-back pass was greeted only by applause), but when someone makes a defensive stop or shares the ball or hustles to get a rebound—demonstrates, that is, that he knows "how the game is supposed to be played"—Schultz stands and high-fives fans around him or makes the raise-the-roof gesture. Desmond Mason effectively defended against a 2-on-1 break, and Schultz not only pumped his fist and cheered Mason but also "saw him the next day and went out of my way to tell him that was the play of the game. He got it."

Schultz also writes encouraging notes to the players that get delivered to their lockers. Schultz was (underperforming and overpaid) forward Vin Baker's principal advocate and encourager, until Baker was traded; "Vin knows I'm not patronizing him," Schultz said—but who said he was? In his occasional column in the *Seattle Times,* Schultz wrote about attending a showcase game for high school stars: "I saw the individual style of play, which has become so rampant in the NBA, where a guy made a great move and then went to center court to perform his own little shimmy dance. These kids have gotten the wrong message: they think that the NBA is more about ego than about teamwork. Today we have more stars than heroes. Basketball at its best is a team sport based on selfless play. As a kid in New York, I remember watching great Knicks games that were all about the players' movements, rhythmic passing of the ball, pick-and-rolls. At the heart of great championship teams is a shared understanding that individual players will sacrifice statistics and self-glorification for the team to win." Asked to name current players he admires, Schultz names the old-style guys: John Stockton (since retired), Karl Malone, Tim Duncan. Life, once, was good; how do we get that feeling back? It's a brilliant shtick because everyone over the age of 12 feels that way. That's why frequently interspersed with the angry lyrics in punk-album liner notes is the beatific child-photograph of the lead singer.

Although Minnesota had one of the best records in the NBA in 2001–2002, the Sonics were the better team on this night and won an entertaining, well-played game, but there were a lot of empty seats: only 11,663 in an arena with a capacity of 17,072.

While NBA attendance was up 1 percent in '01–'02, the Sonics' home attendance was down 14 percent from the previous year— 3,000 fewer fans per game than the NBA average.

Shortly after Schultz's purchase of the Sonics was official, he said, "We'll begin a process of examining all of the practices that go on in this arena—from the time people drive their cars here to the time they leave. I don't want to embrace the status quo. I want to make things better. I've been watching everything the past two or three months. I've seen lightbulbs out on the score-board. Sometimes you can't hear the music. Sometimes you can't see the screen. All of the things that have gone on that I think in any way do not enhance the experience, I want to ask, 'Why?'"

The overwhelming majority of fans I asked about Schultz's Key Arena makeover were oblivious of it or dismissed it as cos-metic, and several fans rang variations on "What I really wish they'd done instead was make a couple of major moves during the off-season." The Sonics were utterly dysfunctional the previous year. The team changed coaches in the middle of the season, and Seattle didn't make the playoffs for the second time in three years. One of the younger Sonics said about the team's veteran, tem-peramental, all-star guard Gary Payton that he better not die because none of his teammates would go to his funeral. Baker, supposedly the second-best player on the team, was hugely depressed, even more hugely overweight, and slogged lethargically up and down the court. And yet almost no substantial personnel changes were made during the off-season. Ruben Patterson, one of the best reserves in the league the previous year, entered a mod-ified guilty plea to third-degree attempted rape over the summer, and the Sonics chose not to re-sign him; when he became a free agent and signed with Portland, the Sonics got nobody in return.

Seattle was reluctant to trade Payton, and unable to trade Baker until the end of the season, so Schultz of necessity trumpeted a newly mature Payton and a newly dedicated Baker. Payton was surprisingly tolerant of his young, erratic teammates, but Baker's weight ballooned and he missed numerous games with minor injuries. The Sonics made the playoffs but were easily eliminated in the first round.

After every game, the new signature song is Bobby Darin's version of "Mack the Knife," which carries, as Schultz said, a "double message": (1) the Sonics coach's nickname is "Mac10"; and (2) what they are trying to do here is escape to a prelapsarian Eden, back in the 1950s, before families split apart and there were angry black people or rap music or sex or money or cable television. Schultz's vision is not dissimilar to that of Ralph Lauren, a middle-class Jewish kid from the Bronx, creating fantasies of the English country gentry; or European Jewish Hollywood moguls, virtually inventing the American dream; or Woody Allen, endlessly romancing the WASP Upper East Side. Starbucks is the antithesis of the diner on every fourth corner of the Upper West Side; Key Arena—milky-smooth, clean as a whistle, as threatening as a warm bath—couldn't be farther from the high school gyms of Schultz's Canarsie boyhood.

As Schultz writes in his 1999 memoir, *Pour Your Heart Into It: How Starbucks Built a Company One Cup at a Time,* "One of the advertising agencies that pitched for our business interviewed Los Angeles–area customers in focus groups. The common thread among the comments was: 'Starbucks is so social. We go to Starbucks stores because of a social feeling.' Yet, strangely, the agency discovered that fewer than ten percent of the people they observed in our stores at any given time actually ever talked to anybody. Most customers waited silently in line and spoke only to the cashier to order a drink." Schultz's gloss: Starbucks customers "felt they were out in the world, in a safe place yet away from the familiar faces they saw every day." His acumen lies in understanding his market. He figured out that we don't truly want the genuine community of a Milan coffee bar. We want upscale, vaguely European ambience in which contemporary culture has been decontextualized and made palatable and attractive to the business class.

SEVERAL HOURS before the Seattle-Minnesota game, High School Pro Sports Day was held at Key Arena. Several hundred kids from Seattle-area high schools came to listen to coaches and executives from the Sonics, the Seattle Storm, and the NBA talk about having a career in professional sports. The kids had on their "all adults suck" expressions; when Schultz's opening joke fell flat, one expected the worst, but then he told them he's from the projects in Brooklyn, his parents "didn't have very much," he grew up in a "lower-class, low-income family, and money was a tough issue." Many of the kids there that day are from similar backgrounds, so they perked up a little. Schultz's mother gave him "a level of self-esteem that was well beyond our means, in convincing all of us—myself, my brother, and my sister—that America was a place where your dreams could come true, if you prepared yourself and you really believed in your dreams and you followed your heart and your passion.

"It's much easier to be successful in life if you are doing something that you truly love, that you're so passionate about it that everyone you touch and everyone you meet recognizes that you will go through a wall, you'll do whatever it takes to get this done, because you love it so much." Schultz had an opportunity to be part of a company that, "believe it or not, changed the world." How did it change the world? It gave all of its employees stock options. "Starbucks is not about coffee. Starbucks is in the people business." Schultz's father "never made more than twenty thousand dollars a year" and "had a series of terrible, terrible jobs throughout his life. He never owned anything. So when we were building Starbucks, the thought that I had was, How could we build the kind of company that my dad never got a chance to work for?" No matter who you are at Starbucks, you "were going to be respected and treated with respect and dignity every day" and "everyone has had an opportunity to participate in our success. The success that we have enjoyed has been very sweet because everyone has shared in it and no one was left behind. The lesson there is that success is best when it is shared."

Which—he explained in his platitude-driven but oddly effective, because so seemingly heart-felt and hard-won, manner—goes the same for the Sonics: "It's important to play in such a way that the ball is shared, there's trust on the court; the game is built not around selfishness but teamwork and team spirit. I've made a promise, to this community as well as to the players and everyone involved, that we are going to return this team back to the NBA elite. And it's going to happen. You're going to tell your friends some day, three years from now or whenever it is, that you were standing in the arena when Howard Schultz said, 'We're going to return this team back to the NBA elite.' And you're going to remember, when the Seattle SuperSonics win the NBA championship. I promise you!"

The place erupted. Baker had said, "When he comes in and

talks to our team, he always wells up. I'm a big crier, too. Howard always wells up when he's speaking to our team, and that's natural. He's not making up tears to talk to our team." Schultz is positively Clintonesque in his ability to feel your pain—to move you by how moved he is by the human drama of your life. He's very good at getting what he wants by imagining what you want and then telling you that.

At the conclusion of what had come to feel more and more alarmingly like a pep rally, Schultz said, "The difference between winning and losing in life, or success and failure, is a very, very thin line. And when you get older than you are right now, there are going to be people in your life—friends, acquaintances, maybe even your parents—who perhaps are going to want you to take the safe road. But don't settle in your life for mediocrity. Because when you get to be twenty-five, thirty, thirty-five, forty years old, you will be miserable if you look back on your life and you say to yourself, 'I should have followed my heart. I should have followed my passion,' and it will be too late. This is a wonderful time in your life. Follow your heart. Follow your dreams. And don't allow *anyone* to talk you out of what is in your heart and what it is you want to do in your life. Believe in yourself and believe in your dreams." Schultz has a nearly obsessive belief in the power of positive thinking, a messianic eagerness to cast himself as the embodiment of the American dream. He has no irony, no apparent self-doubt; selling himself, he sells you. If you haven't gotten inoculated yet, Schultz's ya-gotta-believe earnestness can be contagious.

And the kids went crazy again, though this time in a more somber, sober, reflective way, because what they'd just heard was an Oprah-narrative, and they've been listening to Oprah-narratives since they were two: once, a long time ago, in a land far, far away, but not so very far away after all, there was a strong woman and a weak man and a child, and the child learned from the strong woman and so grew up whole, though still a little wounded, and the wound fuels the drive to succeed, which he does, creating the Willy Wonka Coffee Factory, but then he also repairs the wound, because the Willy Wonka Coffee Factory is about making coffee but really is about making people feel better and being nice to people, even people like his ne'er-do-well father. I once was lost and now am found; follow me: I'll take you—back—to the promised land.

WORDS CAN'T BEGIN TO
DESCRIBE WHAT I'M FEELING

SCHULTZ UNDERSTANDS, IN OTHER WORDS, HOW TO MAKE cliché come out sounding like myth. Sports (as much as any other endeavor is, even as much as political campaigns and book reviews are) is imprisoned by its prevailing rhetoric. The sports narrative goes like this—

I'll be honest with you: I'm here to tell you: The big key is: The bottom line is:

There's no question about it. There's no doubt about it. You got that right. I couldn't agree with you more. Obviously, the statistics speak for themselves.

He's a highly touted freshman. Last week was his coming-out party. He has all the makings of a great one. He has unlimited potential. He's a can't-miss prospect. You'll be hearing a lot from him. He can play at the next level. He can play on Sundays. He's got his whole future ahead of him. He's a youngster who bears watching. He's being groomed for a future starting job. The team is really high on him. He's going to set the world on fire. He's a rookie phenom.

He moves well for a big man. He's sneaky-fast. He has lightning-fast reflexes. He has great lateral mobility. He can pick 'em up and put 'em down. He has both speed and quickness. He's a cutter and a slasher. He has speed to burn. He's fleet-footed. He's a speed merchant. He can fly. He can flat-out fly. Speed kills. You can't teach speed.

He's a unique physical specimen. He has a low center of gravity. He plays bigger than his size. He's built like a brick shithouse. He's a stud. He's a warrior. He's a bulldog. He has a linebacker mentality. He's fearless. He's a physical player. He's an impact player.

He's a tough, hard-nosed player. He's their spark plug. He's their role player. He understands his role on this team. He lets the game come to him. He's the consummate team player. He's an unselfish player. He's a real throwback. He plays with a lot of emotion. He has a passion for the game. He always gives 110 percent. He plays for the name on the front of the jersey, not the name on the back of it.

He's their playmaker. He's their field general. He's their floor general. He's a good table-setter. He's the glue that holds this team together. He makes the players around him better. He's a stand-up guy. The team looks to him for leadership. He's a leader on this team. He's a leader on and off the field.

He's a true professional. He's a professional hitter. He just goes out there and gets the job done. I was just doing my job. I was just hoping I could make a contribution in whatever way they needed me.

He's some kind of player. He's the real deal. He's legit. He can flat-out play. He's as good a player as there is in this league. He's one of the best in the business. He's in a league of his own. He's a franchise player. Players like that don't come along very often. He's a future Hall-of-Famer. He's a first-ballot lock. You can't say enough about him.

He's got ice water running through his veins. He thrives under pressure. He always comes through in the clutch. He really comes through at crunch time. He's their go-to guy when the game's on the line. He's money. He can carry the team on his shoulders. He can take them to the promised land.

He's shooting well from downtown. He's making a living behind the 3-point arc. He's getting some good open looks. He's shooting the lights out. He's in a zone. He's feeling it. He's in a groove. He's lighting it up. He's on fire. He's hot. He's locked in. He's unconscious.

He blew 'em away.

THEY PAY HIM to make those catches. That pass was very catchable. He's usually a sure-handed receiver. He usually makes that catch. He heard footsteps. He's become a little gun-shy. He's got all the skills—he just needs to put them together. He needs to bulk up in the off-season. He needs to elevate his game. He's playing out of position. He lacks the killer instinct.

He's only played sparingly this season. He's the subject of trade rumors. He's being shopped around. He's on the trading block. He's bounced around a lot. He's a journeyman. He's the player to be named later. He's lost a step. He's their elder statesman. I just want to give something back to the community. He's a great role model. He's a winner in the bigger game of life. I just want to be able to take care of myself and my family.

He doesn't have that good fastball today. He's getting by with breaking stuff. He took something off that pitch. He's getting shelled. He's getting rocked. They're teeing off on him. Stick a fork in him—he's done. They need to pull the plug. He hits the showers. Today I didn't have my plus-stuff. Regardless of what kind of stuff you have on a given day, you just try to go out there and pitch to the best of your ability and give your team an opportunity to win.

He got hung out to dry on that play. That was blown coverage. That was a missed assignment. They're playing in the shadow of their goalposts. He couldn't turn the corner. They're looking at third down and forever. They have to establish the running game. They have to air it out more. They have to take care of the football. That missed extra-point could come back to haunt them. You gotta hit the holes they make for you. You gotta follow your blockers out there. He's been quiet so far—they need to get him some more carries in the second half. This is their deepest penetration of the half. They've got to punch it in from here. They can't cough it up here. They need to just go out and make football plays.

He has all the time in the world. He has all day back there. He has all kinds of time. He has an eternity. He threw into double coverage. He threw up a prayer. He'd like to have that one back.

WE JUST couldn't execute. We weren't able to sustain anything. They got us out of our game plan early. They took us completely out of our rhythm.

We got beat like a gong. They beat us like a drum. They out-played us. We ran into a buzz saw. We didn't execute. Turnovers absolutely killed us. We didn't get any calls. Sometimes this game just comes down to the way the ball bounces. We didn't get any breaks. The better team won. They were the better team today. Give them credit. We just didn't get the job done. We weren't mentally prepared. For some reason, they've just got our number. We didn't come to play. They wanted it more than we did. This was a wake-up call. I tip my hat to them. We beat ourselves. We only have to look in the mirror. I don't want to point any fingers. We came up a little short. We had our chances. They outplayed us in every phase of the game. They just made the big plays and we didn't. We dug ourselves a deep hole. We have to put this game behind us. It's going to be a long plane ride home.

THE COACH is on the hot seat. His head is on the chopping block. Unfortunately, there are days like this. We're in the business of winning. It's the nature of this business. It's time to move on. We have to look forward. We need a change of direction. We need a clean slate. We need someone who can take us to the next level.

I feel the time has come for new leadership of this ball club. Everyone has to be held accountable. It's all about winning and losing. I take the blame. I'm not going to stand up here and make excuses. Obviously, I'm disappointed things didn't work out. This is my responsibility and I feel badly I haven't been able to get us going where we should be going. I want to thank our great fans. I'm looking forward to the next chapter in my life. First I'm going to spend more time with my family.

I'm excited about this opportunity. I'm looking forward to

the challenge. I have high expectations for this team. This franchise has a great winning tradition. We've got a good, solid foundation to build on. We're going to right the ship. We're going to get things turned around. This is a great sports town.

THEY STUMBLED coming out of the gate. They got off on the wrong foot. They're finally showing signs of life. They need a late surge. It's been an up-and-down season. It's a marathon, not a sprint.

This team is starting to make some noise. The players have bought into the system. He's got them headed in the right direction. He's a players' coach. He's more of a people person than an X's-and-O's guy. These guys have been busting their tails for him. He gets the most out of his players. They've turned the corner. They've raised the bar. They've gotten over the hump. They've finally gotten off the schneid. They're loaded this year. They have a strong supporting cast. There's no "I" in "team." They've added a new wrinkle to their offense. They're finally getting the respect they deserve. They're for real. They're here to stay. They're playing with new-found confidence. They've got great team chemistry. This team is like a family. Everything's clicking. We're starting to gel. Everybody's on the same page. We're hitting on all cylinders now. Everybody's contributing.

WE'VE GOT THE league's best offense against the league's best defense; something's gotta give. We've got an intriguing matchup. This is a pivotal game. This game is for the bragging rights. These teams flat don't like each other. There's no love lost between these two teams. There's bad blood between these two teams. It's gonna be a war out there. When these two teams get together, you can throw out their records. You have to respect their athleticism. You have to respect their quickness. They have tremendous leaping ability. They can put up big numbers. They do a great job defensively. They play tough D.

They're feeling each other out. Here's the payoff pitch. He chased a bad pitch. Tough to lay off that pitch. 3 up, 3 down. This is shaping up to be a real pitchers' duel. That ball should be playable. It's a can of corn. The ball took a bad hop. Strike-'im-out, throw-'im-out double play. Inning over. He got a good jump. That brings the tying run to the plate. He hits 'em where they ain't. He's a long-ball threat. He hit a solo shot back in the fifth. He's seeing the ball real well. He wears them out. He made good contact. He hit that ball squarely. He hit that ball on the sweet spot. He knocked the cover off the ball. In any other ballpark, that's a home run. Chicks dig the long ball. He's sitting on dead red. He got all of it. He went yard. He hit it into the cheap seats. He flat jacked it. He went deep. He went downtown. Going, going, gone. It's outta here. See ya later. Good-bye, baseball. Kiss it good-bye. Aloha means good-bye.

It's been all theirs to this point. It's theirs to lose. They're not playing to win—they're playing not to lose. They're putting the ball in the deep freeze. Now's the time to run some clock.

Looks like we've got some extracurricular activity going on out there. Let's hope cooler heads prevail. They're mucking it up in the corner. He stood him up on the blue line. That's gotta hurt. He was mugged. He's gonna feel that one on Monday. Looks like we've got a player shaken up. Looks like he got his bell rung. That hit really cleaned his clock. He ran into a brick wall.

He was literally run over by a freight train. He was blindsided. He's slow getting up. He was really clotheslined. They can ill-afford to lose him. Their locker room must look like a MASH unit. X-rays are inconclusive. He left the field under his own power. We hate to speculate on the nature of the injury.

There's a flag on the play. It depends where they spot it. Terrible call, terrible call. We got hosed. We got jobbed. We got robbed. Highway robbery. They're the best refs money can buy. The refs should just let them play. Bad calls even out over the course of a season.

As Yogi said, "It ain't over 'til it's over." It ain't over 'til the fat lady sings. They won't go quietly. We've still got plenty of football left. No need to panic—there's plenty of time left.

You can feel the momentum shifting. Big Mo. They're going for the jugular. They can smell blood in the water. They're within striking distance. Now we've got a football game. It's a whole new ball game. This team shows a lot of character. This team shows a lot of poise. This team shows a lot of resiliency. This team shows a lot of heart.

It all started with good field position. They've marched down the field. That was a goal-scorer's goal. He lit the lamp. He went high to the top shelf. He put the biscuit in the basket. He found the twine. He went upstairs. He nailed the buzzer-beater. She really stuck the landing. He hit pay dirt. Nothing but net. This should be a chip shot for him. The kick splits the uprights.

What an incredible turnaround.

WE FOUND A way to win. A win is a win. It wasn't pretty, but we'll take it. I'm really proud of the way our guys hung in there.

This is always a tough place to play. We're just glad to get out of here with a W. We're happy we could pull this one out at the end. They're tough competitors. They gave us all we could handle. They're a class act. Give them a lot of credit. I tip my hat to them. There are no easy games in this league. The game was a lot closer than the final score indicates. They weren't going to come in here and just lie down for us. We're going to use this as a building block. We'll use this win as a stepping stone to the next level.

What a difference a week makes.

We were really on our game. We took them out of their game. We really came to play. We brought our A-game. We knew what we had to do and went out and did it. We answered the call. This team has finally learned how to win. It was a total team effort. Obviously, this was a great win for us. It was a big win for us. We came to play. We stuck to the game plan. It was a total team effort. We wanted to make a statement. We sent a message. We came through when it counted. We're going to savor the victory tonight, then tomorrow morning we'll start looking at film.

THE ONLY THING that matters in the Stanley Cup playoffs is the man between the pipes. You can't win an NBA championship without a dominant big man. You can't win in the NFL without establishing the run. Offense puts fannies in the seats—defense wins championships. You've got to have pitching if you're going to make it through the postseason.

We just need to go out there and take care of business. It all just comes down to execution. You can't leave anything on the table. We need to bring it. We need to dig deeper than we've ever dug before. We just gotta go out tomorrow and have fun.

They've battled back from the brink of elimination. They're down but not out. They're in a must-win situation. They need a win to stave off elimination. Lose and go home. There's no tomorrow. I know it's a cliché, but we just have to take it one game at a time.

We gotta stick to the basics. We need to remember what got us here. You gotta dance with who brung ya. This is it. This is for all the marbles.

They need to keep up their intensity. They have to stay focused. They have to get after it. They have to rise to the occasion. They've got tremendous mental toughness. They're a blue-collar team. They're overachievers. They've come out of nowhere. They're a real Cinderella story. They have to stay hungry. They're loaded for bear.

The city has rallied around this team. We've got die-hard fans. We feed off the energy of our fans. Our fans are our twelfth man. We've got the greatest fans in the world.

We're happy to be in the postseason, and now we want to go out there and do some damage. We're capable of going deep in the postseason. We're not just happy to be here. This team has a chance to do something special. Hopefully, we can steal one on the road. In the playoffs, anything can happen.

Game time.

The fans are on their feet. This crowd is going wild. This place is a madhouse. This place is pandemonium. You can feel the electricity. Ya gotta love these fans. Ya gotta love this game.

HEAVEN IS A PLAYGROUND

I'M A SUCKER FOR SPORTS MOVIES, THOSE ENGINES OF RIT-ualized truism. Flipping through the channels late at night, I'll come across *The Longest Yard* and not be able to get up off the couch until Burt Reynolds has scored the winning touchdown. Although she'd never expressed the slightest interest in it, I insisted on taking my daughter to see *The Rookie*. (We loved it.) The only screenplay I've ever written is an adaption of that first novel of mine—the one about a sportswriter and the star college basketball player whom he worships and deplores. Why do I have such an affinity for sports movies? Not good sports movies, though, such as *Bang the Drum Slowly*, or great sports movies, such as *Raging Bull*, or melancholy sports movies, such as *North Dallas Forty*, but instead the pure-sugar solution itself: *Hoosiers. Angels in the Outfield. Rookie of the Year. Field of Dreams. For Love of the Game. Ladybugs. Mr. Baseball. Rudy. Rocky. The Natural.*

The Air Up There. Hardball. The Karate Kid. Major League. The Replacements. Why, despite knowing how formulaic these films are, am I invariably moved when watching them, often to the point of tears? What story are they telling that appeals—at least to me—on such a primitive level? And how can the same story get told—why does the same story need to be told—over and over and over?

In *For Love of the Game,* Kevin Costner plays a character named Billy Chapel. In *Downhill Racer,* Robert Redford is David Chappellet. In *Hoosiers,* the player who saves the team is named Jimmy Chitwood. In *He Got Game,* Denzel Washington's son is named Jesus. Sports movies, which need to convince the viewer to care about fictional contests between nonexistent teams, borrow the grammar of resurrection and salvation. Something has to be at stake in the game other than the final score; the script inevitably moves in the direction of religious iconography.

Major League begins by informing the viewer that Cleveland last won the World Series in 1948. *Rookie of the Year* opens with similar information about the Chicago Cubs (last World Series win: 1908). The overture of *Field of Dreams* is the voice-over narrator's ode to his dead father, who nearly made it to the bigs. In *Hoosiers,* we immediately learn that the Indiana high school team Gene Hackman coaches last won the state championship in 1951. Walter Matthau, now a Little League coach in *Bad News Bears,* was once a major-league pitcher. So was Tom Hanks, now coaching a women's team, in *A League of Their Own.* Rocky, as a photo of him on his dresser makes evident, was once a happy kid with light in his eyes; he takes the photo off the mirror and holds it up, comparing what he was to what he's become. Costner, in *For Love of the Game,* was earlier in his career an all-star pitcher—

"golden, one of the giants." The first, crucial gesture many sports movies make is for the protagonist to say, sotto voce or not so sotto voce, to the viewer, "We once strode the earth as gods."

An alternative scenario is that long ago, in the primordial past, the hero fucked up. History is a nightmare from which he is—all of us are—trying to awake. He gets a second chance to come back to life; he better not blow it. In *The Best of Times*, Robin Williams drops a pass in the big game against the high school down the road. He spends the rest of his life being pummeled for this failing and finally gets a chance to redeem himself. In *The Replacements*, Keanu Reeves has never recovered from his mysteriously awful performance in the 1996 Sugar Bowl, but he now gets a chance as a replacement player for the striking pros. Paralleling Reeves's transformation, the disco hit "I Will Survive" goes from locker-room joke to oddly moving anthem of personal redemption and team solidarity.

In either version, we get evicted from paradise. We're lost in a vast desert. *Major League* begins with a vast desert, literally. The team's training camp is in Arizona; a lizard crawls among the cactuses just outside the field. The Indians' roster, in *Major League*, features a voodoo worshipper, a player who can't hit the ball fair, another who can't throw it straight. The play-by-play man is a drunk; the color man never says a word. It's a freak show. It's the lonely hearts' club. In *Field of Dreams*, the wounded warriors on the yellow brick road are a blocked writer, a player who got into only one game and never had an at-bat, a man who never made it to the major leagues, another who was unfairly tarnished by scandal. In *Bad News Bears*, the Little League team is sponsored by Chico's Bail Bonds, and the players are a black kid, an Hispanic kid, a Jewish kid, a fat kid, a shy kid, and a kid who's been abused by his parents, all of whom are mocked by the one WASP kid. The dramatis personae of *The Replacements* includes a deaf-mute, a sumo wrestler, a couple of bodyguards, an insane SWAT-team cop, a wide receiver who can't catch, and a thief. We're living in the land of the damned.

The team is, needless to say, losing. Some of this is simple narrative typology: a romantic comedy can't begin with the lovers in a happy embrace. This goes beyond that, though. In film after film, it's a plague of losing streaks. We're losing. We're losers. We're bums. We're in a state of infinite regress, of existential failure. In the land of opportunity, we are antimatter. In *Slap Shot,* the players are trapped in Pennsylvania's Federal League; in *Bull Durham,* it's minor-league A-ball; in *The Replacements,* they're scabs replacing the real NFL players; in *Field of Dreams,* they're in Iowa, these players forever shadowed by the 1919 Black Sox scandal; in *Rocky,* they're in South Philly; in *Hardball,* they're on the South Side of Chicago; in *For Love of the Game,* they're the Detroit Tigers, a team that has an illustrious past but hasn't won in decades. And they're playing the Yankees, who figure in many baseball films as the Goliath whom David must slay or die trying. These films are, by definition, obsessed with the underside of the American Dream. As a corollary, movies such as *Paper Lion; Mystery, Alaska; Lucas; Tin Cup; Rocky; The Bad News Bears; A League of Their Own;* and *Rudy* are odes to perpetual losers who succeed by the force of their trying; they fail, but their failure is noble because, determined to succeed but overpowered by forces of economics, personal psychology, and body type, they nevertheless get their groove back. We can identify: our body types might not be so ideal, either.

The owners in sports movies are eleven kinds of asshole:

they're money-obsessed; they want to fire the hero; they want to sell the team; they want to move the team to Miami. Why, in so many movies, Miami? It's both heaven (paradisal retreat from the workaday world of, say, *Slap Shot*'s Pennsylvania rustbelt) and hell (retreat and descent from, say, *Slap Shot*'s Pennsylvania rustbelt, which has a heavenly aura once the balm of athletic glory has been applied to it). If the player often becomes a Christ figure, the owner is clearly a stand-in for the Pharisees, the Roman officers, the money-changers. Athletes are in touch with the gods—that's why we love them—but the only god the owner is in touch with is Midas. In movie after movie, the owner's young, voluptuous wife pours alcohol down her throat or stuffs her face with food or stuffs her yappy little dog's face with food because hubby-made-of-money doesn't satisfy in the sack. She wants, implicitly or (in a few films) explicitly, the players, who are "real," or a particular player, who is particularly "real," the irony being that this player is always Paul Newman or Keanu Reeves or Nick Nolte or Kevin Costner or Robert Redford. He's real, but he's a movie star. "He's an animal"; "No, he's a god," as *The Babe* has it.

This suits vs. jocks animus is, in a way, the narrative tension of nearly every sports movie, for these films return again and again to the opposition between the social (which is corrupt) and the body (which is miraculous). The three-act structure of virtually every studio-produced American movie mandates that Plot Point A occurs approximately twenty minutes into the movie. The next hour is usually devoted to the complications that ensue from Plot Point A. Twenty minutes before the end of nearly every Hollywood movie, Plot Point B occurs, which spins the action downward toward its conclusion. In many sports movies—*The*

Natural, Angels in the Outfield, Rookie of the Year, Field of Dreams, Like Mike—Plot Point A is the discovery of the protagonist's magic athletic prowess; in many other sports movies, the magic element is introduced at exactly this same point, but the magic is more figurative. The next hour consists of a conflict between various forces of social corruption and the force of this magical power, and then at the end of the film, the magic is triumphant. The magic, though, is no longer supernatural ability—which has usually dissipated by now (Plot Point B)—but the redemptive power of love.

So the son plays catch with the father, resurrected (in *Field of Dreams*). Our hero pitches a perfect game (in *For Love of the Game*). We win. We win. We win the big game. We reconcile generations, races, the war between the sexy sexes. We win the pennant. We make it to the bigs. We get to play in the big game. We're finally on the interstate; we're no longer trapped on the service roads. We hit the home run. We save the team from bankruptcy, departure, ignominy, collapse. We defeat the bully opponent (the Yankees, the fascistic karate coach). We come together as a team, especially that; we're now all pulling in the same direction. In *Field of Dreams*, Ray's brother-in-law, that Pharisee, that money-changer, tells Ray, "Just sign the papers. Sell now or you'll lose everything. You're broke. When the bank opens in the morning, they'll foreclose." James Earl Jones thunders back, "Ray, people will come [to the baseball field Ray has imagined into existence in his backyard]. They'll come to Iowa for reasons they can't even fathom. They'll turn up your driveway, not knowing for sure why they're doing it. They'll arrive at your door, as innocent as children, longing for the past. . . . And they'll walk off to the bleachers, sit in their shirt sleeves on a perfect afternoon, and they'll find they have reserved seats somewhere along one of the baselines where they sat when they were children and cheered their heroes, and they'll watch the game, and it will be as if they dipped themselves in magic waters."

"Magic waters": baptism, one of the seven sacraments of the Catholic Church, is frequently called the "first sacrament," "the door of the sacraments," and the "door of the church." *Field of Dreams* isn't about Ray Kinsella (Costner) sacrificing his body— he's not an athlete—but baptism is a good way of understanding the movie's signature line, "If you build it, they will come." Ray is building a baseball field, but he's also building a door of the church. Does James Earl Jones die when he walks into the corn-field? The players who show up, including Ray's father, are most certainly dead, but here they are, playing catch. In baptism, we are "buried with him into death," but it's also a "likeness of his resurrection": an immersion, followed by an emersion. "Is this heaven?" Ray's father, John, asks Ray. Ray says, "It's Iowa." "Iowa?" John says. "I could have sworn this was heaven." "Is there a heaven?" Ray asks. "Oh yeah," John replies. "It's the place where dreams come true." Ray, watching his wife play with their daughter on the front porch, says, "Maybe this is heaven." Paradise regained: heaven is a playground. The movie—any sports movie—becomes a praise song to life here on earth, to physical existence itself, beyond striving, beyond economic necessity. I remember a wonderful short story a graduate-school classmate wrote about a bunch of old guys in Florida who go night after night to a porn-movie theater (this was before the advent of videos). Why do they go? To say, "We're here, God, we're still here." I went to graduate school at the Iowa Writers' Workshop; so, a decade earlier, did W. P. Kinsella, who wrote the novel upon which *Field of Dreams* is based. He set his sports fantasy in Iowa City; so did I.

In *Ladybugs,* Rodney Dangerfield protests to his type A boss: "The best, the best—that's all I keep hearing. You want to be the best [by having me coach the boss's daughter's soccer team to the championship]. Well, let me ask you this: What good is being the best if it brings out the worst in you?" What profiteth a man if he gaineth the world but loseth his soul? This is the interesting middle path that nearly all of these films try to walk—finding a way for the protagonist to be successful without the film endorsing a bland Ben Franklin/Jay Gatsby/Horatio Alger/Little Engine That Could ethos of dogged, American striving. The films need to be critiques of win-at-all-costs relentlessness at the same time that they figure out a way for their heroes to succeed. In *Remember the Titans* and *For Love of the Game,* respectively, Denzel Washington's and Kevin Costner's Achilles' heel is shown to be workaholism; by the end of each film, they learn to give a little, to discover the homo ludens gene hidden somewhere still in their psyche, to learn to depend on themselves a bit less and on others a bit more, to cut others some slack; supporting players aren't made of the same stern stuff as the hero, after all. In *Breaking Away,* Dave Stoller doesn't cheat, as the Italian bikers do, but he wins the race with a little help from his friends. In *Mr. Baseball,* Tom Selleck learns from his Japanese teammates that in some circumstances what's called for isn't the American-ish long ball; it's the Japanese-style bunt. In *Hoosiers,* Gene Hackman, unlike the town elders, is willing to let the team lose for the sake of a principle; this very principledness is the source of his and the team's salvation. In *The Karate Kid,* Mr. Miyagi teaches Daniel how to focus not on winning the karate tournament (as the opposing coach, a Vietnam vet, does with his charges) but on thinking seriously and truly about karate; Daniel also wins the tournament, of course. In *The Bad News Bears,* Walter Matthau isn't prepared to go all out to win the big game; it doesn't matter anymore, because the Bears are now bad news to the opposition rather than to themselves. Exactly the same thing happens in *Hardball:* Keanu Reeves's charges lose the final game. Who cares? They're alive again, despite or perhaps because of their saintly teammate Jarius's death. In *Democracy in America,* Alexis de Toqueville writes: "A democracy finds it difficult to coordinate the details of a great undertaking and to fix on some plan and carry it through with determination in spite of obstacles. It has little capacity for combining measures in secret and waiting patiently for the result. Such qualities are more likely to belong to a single man or to an aristocracy." These movies solve the dilemma of democracy—the difficult negotiation between individual striving and egalitarian community—by praising the ragtag team but really praising the charismatic leader who galvanizes the team. Who wouldn't want to be on that team, led by that leader?

Hell is not, then, as it is in the Euro-version, other people, but self, and heaven is team. In Al Pacino's speech to the troops as the coach in *Any Given Sunday,* he says, "We're in hell right now, gentlemen, believe me. And we can stay here—get the shit kicked out of us—or we can fight our way back into the light. We can climb out of hell one inch at a time. And I know if I'm going to have any life anymore it's because I'm still willing to fight and die for that inch. Because that's what living is: the six inches in front of your face. Now, I think you're going to see a guy who will sacrifice himself for this team, because he knows, when it comes down to it, you're going to do the same for him. That's a team, gentlemen, and either we heal now as a team, or we will die as individuals. That's football; that's all it is. Now what are you gonna do?" Our "flaws"—we're selfish, we're drunks, we're divorced, we're separated, we're hotheads, we're kleptomaniacs, we're superstitious, we're drug addicts, we can't throw, can't catch, can't field, can't shoot, can't run, are afraid, are headstrong, are too big, too small, we're women, we're Jewish, we're black, we're fat, we're kids, we're nearsighted, we're poor, we're hicks, we're Americans—are not only overcome but they define us and beatify us, sanctify us. And yet where would the Tin Woodsman, the Scarecrow, and the Cowardly Lion be without Dorothy? Still in Kansas. This team needs a strong—a very strong—leader. And who is this leader? "Ah, buddy. Ah, buddy," as Salinger's Zooey would, or actually does, say. "It's Christ Himself. Christ Himself, buddy."

In *For Love of the Game*, Costner moves from person to person, healing their wounds and absolving them of their sins, not to mention fixing their cars, offering sage advice, dispensing gentle witticisms, and tipping hugely. This debt is repaid in full at the end of the movie when the veteran catcher comes out to the mound in the ninth inning of Costner's perfect game and tells him, "Chappy, you just throw whatever you got left. The boys are all here for you. We'll back you up. We'll be there. We don't stink right now. We're the best team in baseball right now, right this minute, 'cause of you. You're the reason. We're not going to screw that up. We're going to be awesome for you right now. Just throw." Athlete as almsgiver. Christ and his twelve apostles. A shepherd and his sheep. Bathing the team in his love, he makes us better. He loves us into loving ourselves again. Many movies create a nimbus of moral light around the hero, but the pattern here is so insistent as to establish a mini-subgenre: sports movie as passion play. In *Field of Dreams*, Costner (again) must "ease his pain." Whose pain? His father's, but also Shoeless Joe Jackson's, Moonlight Graham's, and Terence Mann's, and ours, ours. Rocky loves people to death or, rather, out of their spiritual death; by the end of the film, he has remade his shy girlfriend, his bitter coach, his unemployed friend. The first image of *Rocky* is of Christ holding a Communion wafer, as if he were a Catholic priest performing the Eucharist sacrament; at the Last Supper, Christ says, "This is my body, which will be given up for you." In the very next shot, Rocky is getting the shit beat out of him. In other movies, athletes sacrifice their bodies by playing with injuries (*Major League, Slap Shot*) or actually dying (*Hardball, Pastime*). The last image of *Rocky* is of Rocky posed as a close approximation of the Pietà. The athlete's bloodied body, given in battle for us, is the crux.

"And a little child shall lead them." Not only the Christ-hero but the lowliest of us needs to come through as well. In *For Love of the Game*, Billy Chapel's best bud, the guy riding shotgun, the journeyman catcher, needs to come through with a big hit in the top of the ninth before Costner completes his perfect game in the bottom of the inning. The King's garments touch everyone, even Jarius in *Hardball*, the littlest of the little, who proves his mettle before being shot by drug runners and in whose honor his teammates play the championship game. At Jarius's funeral, Keanu Reeves says, "With our hopes dwindling, he hit a shot down the first-base line, and we won the game. And watching him raise his arms in triumph as he ran to first base, I swear I was lifted in that moment to a better place. I swear he lifted the world for that moment. He made me a better person, even if just for that moment. I am forever grateful to Jarius [Jesus?] for that." Even Merle, in *Hoosiers,* the minuscule blond cherub, turns into Merlin and magically hits two free throws to propel Hickory into the state championship. Rudy, in *Rudy,* is a boy among men, but he shows the boy-men how to be men. So does Lucas in *Lucas.* The last shall be first.

And yet nearly every sports movie tends to elide the Big Moment. Weirdly, it often seems to just slide by. In part, this is because the structure of the movie is usually based on the rhythm of a season and so the climax of the film is making it to the World Series; there's no time for the seven games of the World Series. So, too, the World Series is heaven on earth, and the movie can't show heaven on earth, so it shows the ascension. The movie got you there: the viewer can imagine the rest (it's better that way). Watching *Field of Dreams,* we really want to know what's on the other side of the cornfield, but we're never fully enlightened.

What the films tend to do for endings instead is to try to extract from the relevant sport the perfect sports metaphor and dilate that. In *The Karate Kid,* Daniel assumes the Crane Posture, which Mr. Miyagi had taught him early on and the value of which Daniel never understood; using it now, in the final moments of the karate championship, he seems to have gathered all that Mr. Miyagi has taught him and not only absorbed it as philosophy but used it as winning strategy. So, too, in *Personal Best*—a film about two female track stars, Mariel Hemingway and Patrice Donnelly, who become friends, lovers, antagonists, and friends again; at the end of the film, Hemingway sacrifices herself by running out to a lead too early and then creating an opening, a gap, a space (a female space) through which Donnelly can pass and thus join her friend in qualifying for the Olympics. The movie doesn't show the Olympics; it shows the striving. Sports movies are often very good at dramatizing this intersection of public and private realms: the body politic.

"Adrian!" Rocky shouts. "Adrian! Adrian!" Surrounded by admirers after he's lasted fifteen rounds with Apollo Creed, Rocky wants only to see his beloved. The ending of innumerable sports movies replicates this moment: the applause of the crowd must be there, but once there, it's deemed inconsequential, background noise. This is analagous to being in a movie audience and wanting to be with that audience, needing the human heat of a crowd, but also needing to commune with the screen in a private, rhapsodic way, just you and the star. You and the crowd; then you and the star. Also, you and your sweetheart, and you and the world. Agape and Eros. You want the world to love you, but then you want someone to be there to love you while the world is loving you, so the two of you can tell yourself that the world's admiration doesn't matter. Which it does and which it doesn't.

So far I've tried, I suppose, to maintain a certain exegetical distance toward the mythic structure of feel-good sports movies, but listen to this: the actor Craig T. Nelson bought the rights to that first novel of mine and hired me to adapt the book into a screenplay, though the movie never got made. Over the years, I kept tinkering with the script, at one point reducing it to a fifteen-page "treatment" (synopsis). I just pulled it out of a drawer, and whaddya know? The losing team, the town in the toilet. The shepherd leading his sheep to the Land of Oz. Becoming successful but rejecting win-at-all-costs. And a little child shall lead them. Agape and Eros. The elision of the big moment. The perfect sports metaphor. The praise song to existence here, now, on earth, beyond worldly care. Virtually every sports-movie motif that I've tracked in this essay I found in full force in my synopsis, written many years ago. I'd never particularly gone to school on these movies, until now. Which suggests that (a) I've watched way too many sports movies over the years; (b) I have or had an embarrassingly formulaic imagination; or (c) this narrative is simply part of the culture and that we (men especially, since men don't give birth; women already suffer physically to give life to us all) will forever be drawn to it, this lullaby of salvation told by and about the body.

FANDOM

SPEAKING OF WHICH: IN GRADUATE SCHOOL, IN IOWA CITY, I was utterly devoted to one thing: the University of Iowa basketball team. A well-known writer—say, Joseph Heller—would give a reading on the same night as a big game—say, the Iowa-Indiana game—and I wouldn't even have to wonder about which event I'd be attending. My closest friend at Iowa, Philip, liked to say he wouldn't have survived adolescence without Walt Frazier. Every night, he'd hear his mother and father screaming at each other in the next room, and he'd just stare at the Knicks game on the little black-and-white TV at the edge of his bed, trying to will himself into "Clyde's" body. In the spring of 1980, when Iowa beat Georgetown to advance to the Final Four, Philip and I jumped up and down and cried and hugged each other in a way we wouldn't have dreamed of doing otherwise.

Twenty years later, both Philip and I live in Seattle. Our team is now the Seattle SuperSonics, and whenever he and I watch their games on TV, Philip seems to go out of his way to compliment good plays by the other team, and I always want to ask him: Is it a conscious effort on your part to not succumb to jingoistic cheering, or are you constitutionally incapable of the monomania required? I admire his equanimity, but I can't even pretend to emulate it. Unable to say exactly what the disease is, I want the Sonics to cure me.

Sports passion is deeply, infamously territorial: our city-state is better than your city-state because our city-state's team beat your city-state's team. My attachment to the Sonics is approximately the reverse of this. I've lived here for less than a third of my life, and none of the players are originally from the Northwest, let alone Seattle. I revel in our non-Seattle-ness. My particular demigod is (or was, until he was traded) Sonics point guard Gary Payton, who's one of the most notorious trash-talkers in the NBA. He's not really bad. He's only pretend-bad—I know that—but he allows me to fantasize about being bad.

Which is weirdly important to me here because the ruling ethos of Seattle is forlorn apology for our animal impulses. When I castigated a contractor for using the phrase "Jew me down," he returned later that evening to beg my forgiveness, and the next week he mailed me a mea culpa and a rebate. Seattleites use their seat belts more, return lost wallets more, and recycle their trash more than people do in any other city. The Republican (losing) candidate for mayor was the man who (allegedly) invented the happy face. Last month, an old crone wagged her finger at me not for jaywalking but for placing one foot off the curb while she drove past, and my first and only thought was: this is why I love the Sonics; this is why I love Gary Payton.

Growing up, I was a baseball fan. My father and I shared an obsession with the Dodgers (he was born in Brooklyn and I was born in L.A.), and recently I asked him why he thought the team was so crucial to us. He wrote back, "For me, it comes out this way: I wanted the Dodgers to compensate for some of the unrealized goals in my career. If I wasn't winning my battle to succeed in newspapering, union-organizing, or whatever I turned to in my wholly unplanned, anarchic life, then my surrogates—the nine boys in blue—could win against the Giants, Pirates, et al. Farfetched? Maybe so. But I think it has some validity. In my case. Not in yours." Oh, no: not in my case, never in mine. Sometimes what being a fan seems to be most about is nothing more or less than self-defeat.

For me, baseball and the Dodgers have been supplanted by basketball and the Sonics. The basketball high is quicker and sharper. In fact, the oddest thing about it is how instantaneously the game can move me, like a virus I catch upon contact. In a fraction of a second, I'm running streaks down my face. It's a safe love, this love, this semi-self-love, this fandom. It's a frenzy in a vacuum—a completely imaginary love affair in which the beloved is forever larger than life.

I live across the street from a fundamentalist church, and whenever the Sonics play particularly well, I'm filled with empathy for the churchgoers. They go to church, I sometimes think, for the same reason fans go to games: adulthood didn't turn out to have quite as much glory as we thought it would; for an hour or two, we're in touch with something majestic.

The psychoanalyst Robert Stoller has written, "The major traumas and frustrations of early life are reproduced in the fantasies and behaviors that make up adult erotism, but the story now ends happily. This time, we win. In other words, the adult erotic behavior contains the early trauma. The two fit: the details of the adult script tell what happened to the child." This seems to me true not only of sexual imagination but also of sports passion—why we become such devoted fans of the performances of strangers. For once, we hope, the breaks will go our way; we'll love our life now; this time we'll win.

HISTORY OF AMERICA, #34

ACTUALLY, THIS TIME WE'LL LOSE AGAIN, BUT WE'LL PHRASE it as victory: the question before the court is, Why does Charles Barkley—NBA superstar turned television commentator—have, in the words of his TNT colleague Ernie Johnson, "diplomatic immunity"? Why does Barkley get to say virtually whatever he wants (criticize anyone, anything) whereas, for instance, the producers of *Barbershop* are forced to apologize for having a fictional character call Martin Luther King a "ho"? Barkley says it's because he's consistent: "You know I'm going to praise you if you do good, and I'm gonna criticize you if you do bad"—which actually has very little to do with it. Johnson says, "I think it's because his softer side is well known"—which has more to do with it. Turner Sports president Mark Lazarus says, "He can straddle that line without going over it"—which has even more to do with it.

Dave Coskey, the Philadelphia 76ers' director of public relations when Barkley played there, said, "Most of these guys are jerks who want you to think they're nice guys. But Charles is a genuinely nice guy who wants you to think he's a jerk." In *Look Who's Talking Now* (1993), a little girl, age 3, watches over and over a tape of Barkley playing basketball. She carries around a Barkley doll and is infatuated with him. In her daydream, she plays basketball with him and he is her best friend and perfect role model; he even lets her beat him. The fantasy worked because it contradicted Barkley's bad-boy persona at the time but conformed to what we intuited about him more deeply. Why was it so funny when, a decade ago on *Saturday Night Live*, Barkley played a game of one-on-one against Barney the purple dinosaur and wound up punching Barney's lights out? Because we all know Barkley is Barney. His tail bent and one eyeball dangling from its socket, Barney said, "Charles told me I'm special."

Sports Illustrated once called Charles Barkley "Alan Keyes with monster ups." The ups are over. Barkley now weighs 300 pounds; his immensity is crucial to us loving him so much. Imagine a whippet-thin Oprah. It doesn't work. She needs to be suffering from, or at least appear to be suffering from, the same issues she's discussing with her demographic. In America we need our wizards to come in warm/cuddly packages. As he likes to remind himself and us, Barkley is worth $35 million. No one ever got rich truly discomfiting the populace. Madonna sticking out her tits and scolding us for staring—that much feminism we can handle. In the same way, Barkley is the reassuring rebel, the candid huggy-bear, a weird admixture of Muhammad Ali and George Foreman. Barkley's race-anger is exactly the amount of race-anger we can process, which is to say: not that much. He's a race-man of nearly nineteenth-century vintage: he believes in everybody pulling himself up by his own bootstraps. Apotheosizing Charles Barkley is the only reparation we're going to be handing out this year; white America needs to know that beneath all that black rage is, finally, forgiveness, even love. Barkley is proof.

BARKLEY'S BOOK *I May Be Wrong but I Doubt It* was dictated to *Washington Post* sportswriter Michael Wilbon and published by Random House in 2002; the press release for the book compared Barkley to Bill O'Reilly and Molly Ivins. Barkley has nothing in common with such ideologues, but it's instructive that the publicity department would compare him to someone on the right and someone on the left, since Barkley's appeal is, precisely, that he transcends political labels, that for all his storm and noise, he's resolutely middle-of-the-road. On the book-tour, when pressed, he inevitably settled for the medium-range jumper. On CNN's *Talkback,* asked for his response to Harry Belafonte calling Colin Powell, in effect, a "house nigger," Barkley said, "Well, it's unfortunate because I love Colin Powell. He's one of my heroes. He's somebody I really admire. I honestly have great respect for Mr. Belafonte also." Asked about characters in *Barbershop* making fun of Rosa Parks, Jesse Jackson, and Martin Luther King, Barkley said, "I had no problem with the movie. I wish they hadn't said the thing about Dr. King or Rosa Parks. But I'm smart enough to know that it's just comedy." Asked whether women deserve to be members at Augusta National Golf Course, Barkley said, "No, because it's a private club. It's not a public place. Most of the golf courses I play have no black members, a lot of them don't have Jewish members, and some of them don't have women. They don't want them. I mean, that is the ultimate good-ole-boy net-work." Not exactly *The Fire Next Time*. It's his revolution, not the white liberal's dream version (of the black man's revolution).

Fellow Arizonan John McCain blurbed Barkley's book: "Whether you think he's right or wrong, you'll never find Charles Barkley dull, evasive, or afraid. He's blunt, honest, and funny as hell, a man with strong convictions and a determination to express them without fear of offending the sensibilities of more timid souls. He's got guts, and there's as much to admire in this book as there is in the man." As many blurbs are, it's a (flattering) self-portrait in a convex mirror; it's at least as much about McCain as it is about Barkley, and it captures how it doesn't exactly matter what Barkley says: he's mastered the televisual style of controversy sans consequence, of playing both ends against the middle, of the cult of personality. He once said, "My goal in life is to be president." Asked what his agenda would be, he said, "Lock up everybody over twelve and let kids rule the world." He *is* Barney. Paul Westphal, his former coach, called him "a free spirit—John Wayne in short pants."

Westphal, a friend of Rush Limbaugh's, also said about Barkley, "He enjoys life. He believes all people are equal. He believes in reaping rewards for hard work. That ain't liberal. In fact, he's the very definition of a modern conservative." Quizzed by Robert Novak, on CNN's *Crosstalk,* as to whether he was a Republican or a Democrat, Barkley said, "I'm not either, to be honest with you. I made a joke with my grandmother one time. I was asking her, why are we Democrats? She said, 'Republicans are only for rich people.' And I said, 'I'm rich.' And she hasn't given me a viable answer." The person he'd most like to meet is Colin Powell. After spending four hours with Clarence Thomas, he said, "I think I'm smart, but I was learning on the go talking with him. He's achieved true greatness." Many years ago, he said, "I look at all my old friends in the 'hood and they're in the same place they've always been. On welfare, mostly. All the liberals have done is give the black man an inferiority complex. They gave us a little fish, instead of teaching us how to fish."

And yet, asked what the Republicans might do differently, he said, "I don't know. Actually, to tell you the truth, I have no idea." Explaining why he's never voted in his life, he said, "My one vote isn't going to mean much." Asked why he didn't vote in Arizona, he said, "I don't think it's fair for me to vote in Arizona, because I won't be here that long. I don't have time to keep up with all the issues. I don't vote in Alabama, because I don't keep up with everything there." He's political without being political. He's a bull in a china shop who respects the china shop. Here's really why Barkley doesn't vote: "You're voting for who'll do the best for you, and I don't like that system. You should vote to help everybody." People are good; the system is fucked. This is what everybody responds to in Barkley: his largeness is largesse.

THE WHITE MAN'S simultaneous dream date and nightmare, Barkley improvises in ways that leave most white people flat-footed and half-witted. What do you say to a racial barb that's half-joke, half-truth? Most white boys don't joke back. Asked many years ago if he would ever play again for the 76ers, he said, "I can be bought. If they paid me enough, I'd work for the Klan." In Australia, Barkley, watching someone put a million dollars worth of rubies on a table, said, "Damn, must not be any black folks in Australia. You can't just leave a million dollars worth of jewelry lying around the 'hood." When he got in trouble with the NAACP for saying this, he explained that he sometimes says to whites getting their groove on: "Man, there's nothing in the world that makes me as nervous as seeing white people dance." When a reporter friend asked him about groupies in the NBA, he responded by saying, "That's why I hate white people." When he injured himself in his last season, cutting short his career, he said, "Just what America needs: one more unemployed black man." After that game, walking into the interview room and sitting down next to his 73-year-old grandmother, he said, "Well, guys, I guess this means sex is out of the question tonight." Asked why blacks excel at basketball, he said, "It doesn't cost anything to play." Are these comments meant to reinforce stereotypes that white people have of black people or to mock these stereotypes? It's impossible to tell, which is what gives them their (mild) frisson. We want to tell ourselves we're grappling with racial history and reality when we're really not, and Barkley wittily keeps the issues afloat without ever making them unduly burdensome. He gets what he wants: a raison d'être; and we get what we need: our guilt assuaged.

In *I May Be Wrong,* Barkley's discussions of race tend to be so evenhanded as to pat everyone on the back. He says, "The hardest but most important thing is to get a dialogue going on racial issues. I think people want to do better, I really do. I just think they're afraid. Nobody wants to make the first move. We can't get past worrying about disagreement, so we don't have meaningful conversations to make a difference. Damn, to me there's a lot worse than disagreeing with each other. What's worse, people hating and acting on that hate, or disagreeing?" Regarding the South Carolina flag flap, he says, "I'm not saying I don't understand why people are upset with state flags that include the Confederate flag. It's just that those people are not going to change what they feel in their hearts because they take the flag down. I understand the power of symbols, and if I had anything on my house that seriously offended someone, I'd take it down if for no other reason than common courtesy." Barkley's likable impulse is to find common ground, then to wonder ingenuously why we can't all just get along.

Even this degree of truth-dealing is unimaginable to Michael Jordan, who, when asked why he didn't endorse the black Democratic candidate Harvey Gantt against Jesse Helms, said, "Republicans buy Nikes, too." Barkley seems antiestablishment primarily in contrast to the ultimate establishmentarian Jordan, Barkley's career-long rival and close friend. Jordan once scolded Barkley for wearing a sweater rather than a suit: "Are you trying to look like a basketball player, or do you want to appeal to corporate America?" When Jordan saw Barkley giving money to a homeless person, Jordan grabbed him and said, "Quit doing that. If they're able to ask you for some spare change, they can say, 'Welcome to McDonald's. Can I help you, please?'" Jordan says, "Charles says what's on his mind. He never holds his tongue. I like him because it's like I'm the good brother and he's the bad brother. He says a lot of things the good brother wants to say, but doesn't. And I like that. I know I'm always laughing when we're together." Of course he's laughing: in *Space Jam,* a cartoon paean to Jordan, Jordan's dog is named Charles. Barkley is the voice of the dog, whose talent gets stolen. He's sad: he has no place in the world to go because he can't play basketball. Girls tell him he can't play with them, either. He promises a shrink that he won't swear, won't trash-talk, won't even go out with Madonna, and he winds up getting his talent back. The movie appears to be a cautionary tale of some sort.

Barkley has said that the difference between the public perception of himself and Jordan and the private reality of himself and Jordan is the difference between night and day. This is a slightly oblique way of saying that Jordan is actually the bad brother and Barkley is the good brother. "I understand what Michael is doing," Barkley said when they were both playing in the NBA, "but that's not me. These are my glory days. I'm not going to spend them locked inside some room." Put simply, Barkley loves himself—his former teammate Derek Smith once said, "Charles Barkley is a bigger fan of Charles Barkley's than any other person in the world"—but (unlike, say, Jordan) he also seems to love other people, find other people interesting. He's as much a social creature as Bill Clinton, whom on *Crosstalk* Barkley called the best president America's had in Barkley's lifetime (never mind that Barkley is or was or sometimes is a Republican). "His heart is what makes him so great," a coach once said about him. In *I May Be Wrong,* he says that after 9/11, people finally understood what he has been trying to say all along: "There's no black, there's no white, there's no liberal, there's no conservative. We all want the same things in life. We're all the same, and we got to do something about it." "I've had plenty of people tell me it appears I enjoy being famous," Barkley said recently. "But I've always disagreed with that. It's that I enjoy meeting people. There are only two ways to go about life if you're famous: enjoy this damn life or be miserable. I just refuse to stop living my life and enjoying great restaurants or hanging out with friends because I'm a public person. To me, one of the great things in life is to go out and meet new people, people whose experiences are different from your own. It has nothing to do with being recognized and well known." Regarding his experience in the 1992 Olympics, he said, "I loved Barcelona. Loved it. Maybe some people don't enjoy that, but I do. I know there are times I've been walking around a city overseas, 10,000 miles from home, and I've thought, 'Here I am, this little kid from Leeds, Alabama, and I'm in Barcelona or Paris or Tokyo." Who wouldn't find this irresistible? No one does. He once changed a stranger's tire, drove him home, then waited until the man's children arrived home from school so they'd believe that Barkley changed their father's tire. At a hotel in Atlanta where he stays for his TNT gigs, a clerk (whom Barkley greeted with a "Hello, girl!") said, "Before I knew him, I thought he was just a big shot with a big mouth. But he's the nicest man in the world."

HE'S ALSO VERY, very hungry. As a TNT commentator, he's an omnivore: no team, no team's player, and certainly no team's concession stand can escape his mouth. When studio host Ernie Johnson, game analyst Kenny Smith, and Barkley were discussing cooking one night, Barkley wondered, "How come y'all call white guys chefs and black guys cooks?" Another time, Johnson, Smith, and Barkley were announcing the game courtside rather than analyzing it from the studio; when the camera cut to them on the sideline, Barkley was eating a huge bag of popcorn while talking at the same time. The conversation then turned to Barkley's culinary proclivities (basically, anything) instead of the game. Smith and Barkley had a bet that Barkley couldn't get under 300 pounds by a certain day toward the end of the 2002 season. On a halftime segment, Barkley stripped down to his shorts and weighed in (at 299). He loves his body and so do Johnson and Smith. His quips follow from his oral satiation quotient (unreachable). For Barkley, hate is worse than overeating. He won't let any single issue destroy his love of love, or his life.

"My momma told me long ago to let my emotions out," he said, and does. "I believe in expressing what you feel. There are people who hide everything inside, and it's guys like that who kill whole families." Praising the sportswriter Rick Reilly, Barkley said, "The more you talk about the truth—even if it's about society, racism, politics—the more his eyes kind of lock in on you. He seems like he's actually interested in what you're trying to say." This is Barkley, too, of course: when reporters ask him questions, you can see the light in his eyes rather than the gun-metal gray that 99 percent of athletes favor. Former Boston Celtics coach Chris Ford said, "I love Charles because he's so honest. You can see a thought form in his head and then move right out of his mouth without stopping in between." He's barkly; he needs to bark: "I think I have an obligation to myself and to God to tell the truth. Whether people take it good or bad, that's not my worry. I think people should say to themselves, 'Is Charles telling the truth?' instead of worrying about who it offends." When Barkley was recently eating in a fashionable restaurant in Atlanta, a dozen 12-year-old girls walked in, all wearing fancy new braids; the birthday girl's mother told Barkley that her daughter's birthday present had been a group trip to the salon. "Whatever happened to Chuck E. Cheese?" Barkley asked the girl's mother. "Ain't no Dairy Queens in Atlanta?" This is Barkley's role in the culture or at least sports culture—bringing us crashing back down to earthly reality. About current NBA players, Barkley said, "They run like deer, jump like deer, and think like deer."

Informed by a British journalist during the 1992 Olympics that the other teams think the U.S. can win just by showing up, Barkley replied, "I think those other teams got a point." "I don't want to kiss anyone's behind," he says. "I don't want to lie to the media. I don't want to lie to anybody. You ask me a question, I'll tell you the truth. You don't like it? Tough shit."

Which isn't to say Barkley isn't also full of shit himself, full of hypocrisies or at least extreme contradictions. He's both truth-teller and scam artist, purveyor of old-school values with new-school style, a social conservative who throughout his playing career was a devotee of strip clubs, an anti-authority authoritarian, a rebel reactionary. After a difficult loss, he once said he felt like going home and beating his wife—the same woman who he said made him cry every time they made love. He's a relentless capitalist whose principal shtick is sticking up for the poor and downtrodden. In the notorious *Sports Illustrated* cover article of a few years ago, for which he posed breaking out of slave's chains, he said, "Sports are a detriment to blacks, not a positive. You have a society now where every black kid in the country thinks the only way he can be successful is through athletics." Yet he is one of the very most omnipresent commercials for this idea of success-through-sports. Barkley, who has said repeatedly that if he ever runs for political office, his primary issue would be improving public education, especially for poor kids, especially for poor black kids, never graduated from college and didn't graduate from high school, either, refusing to complete a Spanish class he found irrelevant. He's perhaps most famous for saying, "I am not paid to be a role model. I am paid to wreak havoc on a basketball court. Parents should be role models. Just because I can dunk a basketball, that doesn't mean I should raise your kids"; it's difficult to think of a recent athlete who is actually more of a role model. Although he was named one of the fifty greatest players in the history of the NBA, his appeal is heavily dependent upon people understanding him to be a gallant loser who could never quite win the big game; he never got the brass ring while Michael Jordan has six and Magic Johnson five. He was one of the fattest players ever to play in the NBA, but his single most important asset was how quickly he could jump. He's large. He contains multitudes. His contradictions don't mean he's dishonest; all of his contradictions are ours as well.

The biggest contradiction: America is God-haunted and godless, and so is he. He's frequently said, "I think God is in my body"—according to his mother, the result of a blood transfusion to his foot when he was 3 months old. But he once asked the devout, poor-shooting A. C. Green, "If God's so good, how come he didn't give you a jump shot?" And, even more ambiguously, he says, toward the end of *I May Be Wrong,* "It's not like religion isn't part of my life, because it is. I grew up going to church. I believe in prayer and treating people the way you would want to be treated. Religion, to me, is your individual relationship with God, or whatever you call your Supreme Being. That's it, plain and simple." This sounds as if he's talking, or trying to talk, himself into the theological position, especially when he then quotes an agnostic friend, who asked him, "How is it then when something bad happens you never acknowledge God?" Barkley's response: "That really made me think. I said, 'That's fair. I don't know the answer, but that's fair.'"

He's preternaturally alert to death's siren, or at least more preternaturally alert than most 40-year-old multimillionaire exathletes are. He wants, desperately, not to waste his life: "I think you have to live as if tomorrow isn't promised to you." A large part of Barkley's appeal is that he feels this to the bottom of his bones, and people can feel that he feels this, and they want some of that. He's alive, here, on this planet, right now. He's a brilliant extemporizer, inside the moment, satyrlike, actively searching for the jugular of truth, and—this is key to presenting moderation in an immoderate appetite—nearly always finding it in humor. Even when he misses the truth, he recognizes the moment's need for something to be said directly about it, even if it's just Barkley, bored, saying, "This sucks." If he were ever to run for office, he'd be constrained by certain ideologies, whereas now he can contradict himself every other day or every other game, can recharge any moment with meaning, whether it's a racial incident or the analysis of a back screen. "There's nobody—nobody—who knows me and doesn't like me," he once said. Apparently true. After his Phoenix Suns lost the world championship to the Chicago Bulls in 1993, he said, "I'm *still* going to Disney World." Aren't we all.

HOW IT FEELS TO BE A PROBLEM

To the real question, How does it feel
to be a problem? I answer seldom a word.

—W. E. B. DuBois

PEOPLE SAID THE 1999 NBA FINALS MATCHUP BETWEEN THE
New York Knicks and the San Antonio Spurs was about speed
versus size or fastbreak basketball versus post-up basketball or
East versus West or metropolis versus podunk. With almost
comic explicitness and near-perfect symmetry, with a symbolism
approximately as oblique as that of *Rocky* or *Hoosiers,* the Finals
were really about two (opposed, dichotomous, essentializing)
ways of being a black man in America. *Gangsta. Good Negro.*
Charles Barkley redux. . . .

Two days after the Finals, I heard a San Antonio Spurs fan say
to an ESPN Sports Radio talk-show host who is a Knicks fan:

"[Marcus] Camby [the Knicks' then center, who is skinny and has tattoos] looked like he just got out of a concentration camp. You got an $84-million slave [Larry Johnson, who called himself and his teammates "rebellious slaves"]. Latrine [Latrell Sprewell] is a nauseating excuse for an athlete. The Knicks are gangsters, basically. I'll never know how guys like that can be allowed to stay in the league. They should all be in jail. The Spurs are classy gentlemen. The Knicks—they're all just about the ho's."

Between games 3 and 4, Larry Johnson, frustrated by his injured knee and poor play, cursed at a member of the NBA's public-relations staff (an African-American woman, it was widely noted—*he's mean to everybody!*) who asked him to fulfill his obligation of meeting with reporters. He was fined $25,000, and the Knicks were fined another $25,000. When Johnson finally did agree to talk to the press, he said his motto was "Fuck the world." The NBC sportscaster Bill Walton called Johnson "a disgrace and a sad human being." Johnson, newly converted to Islam, said Walton "should check his history and see how many slaves his ancestors had."

The same day that I was listening to ESPN Radio, I heard another sports-talk caller ask, with genuine worry in his voice, "Can nice guys like David Robinson and Tim Duncan even be marketed anymore?" It's not an uninteresting question, since Duncan was easily the best player in the series, but he was absolutely imperturbable, Buddhistically detached, cool beyond cool. Asked before Game 3 for his reaction to Madison Square Garden—he was expected to say that he was "intimidated" by coming to the "mecca of basketball"—he instead just shrugged and said, "Nice rims." When San Antonio won the championship, all the other Spurs celebrated exuberantly; Duncan pulled out his mini-camcorder and took home movies. Was his uncanny self-possession of interest to fans? Not many. I'm not sure we go to the NBA Finals to witness the peace that passeth understanding.

DURING HALFTIME of the third game of the series, Peter Vecsey, interviewing Latrell Sprewell on NBC, said he'd love to hear what sort of trash-talking Sprewell used to do with Michael Jordan. Sprewell deflected the question.

Vecsey felt it incumbent upon himself to ask Sprewell whether he understood that if the Knicks won the championship, he'd be as big in New York as Walt Frazier once was. Sprewell again, wisely, declined to answer. Vecsey was trying to make sure that Sprewell understood that this wasn't just a game; it was about something really quite significant: hype.

During the interview with Vecsey, Sprewell wore large, black, rectangular, "library-style" glasses. Who had ever seen him wearing glasses before? Watching the interview, watching it over and over again on tape, I was dying to know whether the glasses were real, though even if they are real, surely his agent conjured them up to signify that Spree is not only a physical being (a gifted athlete who once choked his coach) but a mental one as well (he's a thoughtful, reflective, and articulate man whose hobby happens to be fixing old stereos). Is this fair, though, on my part? Maybe Sprewell just likes wearing glasses when he's not playing. Or maybe he came up with the marketing strategy himself. In any case, it's there as pure subtext—*How cerebral is this physically blessed/cursed black man?*—which everyone is aware of and which no one talks about in public. Sprewell's glasses go right to the mind/body split that is a governing metaphor of racism.

• • •

THROUGHOUT THE series there was quite a lot of discussion about roles, which is code for *Are you a contributing member of society or are you a barbarian?* The Spurs' David Robinson was willing to sacrifice for the good of the team, yielding the starring role to his younger and more talented teammate, Tim Duncan. Robinson played well throughout the series, blocking shots, getting rebounds, scoring modestly, but Duncan was spectacular, with his beautiful bank shots from way out on the floor and his unstoppable jump hooks. "I guess I just figured winning was more important than anything else I could do for the team," Robinson said. "You dream about having a team where everybody trusts each other, all the way, and here we are." *David Robinson is good. He is a good Negro. America is bigger than the sum of its parts.* The Knicks' center Patrick Ewing (since retired), who was injured and sat morosely on the bench in street clothes throughout the series, was asked afterward if next year he'd be ready to do what David Robinson did—give up some shots, as Robinson did for Duncan—and Ewing replied, "My role doesn't change. I'm tired of hearing how the team is better off without me, and all that stuff. What did Robinson do? He gave up shots. I gave up shots. And on that note, you all have a nice day." *Patrick Ewing doesn't get it. America is nothing but the sum of its separate, selfish parts.*

THERE WERE ONLY two white players on either team who got even the most limited playing time—Steve Kerr of the Spurs and Chris Dudley of the Knicks. Both were toward the end of their careers, and both were painfully slow afoot to begin with, but neither of them ever caught a break from the refs. Both Dudley and Kerr seemed to be called for far more than their share of fouls. I happen to know Kerr's mother-in-law, and I spoke to Kerr on the phone a couple of times, asking if he'd be willing to talk to me about all this; he claimed to be interested in discussing the topic, but whenever we planned to meet, he always found he was pressed for time and couldn't talk, gotta go, call me at this other number, let's talk later.

ALTHOUGH MOST of the Knicks gathered for a brief prayer on the court after every game—win or lose—the Spurs were understood to be the God Squad. When, as cocaptain of the Spurs, David Robinson received the championship trophy, he said, "One thing I learned to do this year was trust the Lord through the whole thing. He blessed me, He blessed the team, He took us to the top, and if you learn anything from this, baby, learn that the Lord doesn't give up on His people, baby. He takes you all the way." This was supposedly a spontaneous outpouring of religious fervor, but every time I rewound the videotape and watched Robinson say these words, I was struck mainly by how utterly rehearsed the speech sounded. So, too, Robinson, who gives away a large percentage of his income through his charities Feed My Sheep and The Ruth Project, was much praised for saying, "If I'm clutching on to my money with both hands, how can I be free to hug my wife and kids?" The effectiveness of the statement, sweet as it is, is dependent upon no one having the temerity to wonder whether it's actually Robinson's consciousness or whether his consciousness has been provided to him by a Christian ministry. So I'm going to have the temerity to wonder about it here, but I feel bad about it, I really do. *All right, then, I'll go to hell.*

AFTER THE SPURS beat the Knicks in Game 4, Knicks coach Jeff Van Gundy said, "Their size beat our speed and quickness tonight. Size does matter in this league." *Size does matter?* It seems unbelievably strange to me that, in the racial/sexual amphitheater of the NBA, a white coach would be so tone-deaf as to say this, but, again, maybe it's just me.

During the Finals, a commercial appeared for a tongue-in-cheek science-fiction movie about crime fighters called *Mystery Men:* we see from the waist up a young, naked black man with dyed blond hair (Dennis Rodman Lite?) who, thinking he's invisible, says, "I'm invisible. Can you see me?" Ben Stiller looks with awe at Dennis Rodman Lite's penis and says, "Wow." Clearly, DRL is not invisible. Janeane Garofalo, Stiller's crime-fighting cohort, says to DRL, "Maybe you should put some shorts on or something if you want to keep fighting evil today." Before the ironic, self-aware young white man and white woman can go out to do good today, they first need to sublimate their sexuality (embodied as a hung black man), but in order to sell the movie, sexuality (embodied as a hung black man) needs to become, magically, both visible and invisible, available and off-limits.

In a Nike commercial that ran constantly throughout the Finals, two young, black NBA stars, Kevin Garnett and Shareef Abdur-Rahim, are instructors at Camp Flight. They stand on a very high diving board and teach teenagers how to jump across the width of a swimming pool in order to dunk the ball into a hoop at the other end. "To master hang time, you gotta make the air your friend," Garnett tells the campers. "Jump out there and shake hands with the alley-oop," Abdur-Rahim says. All of the kids fail this surreal task, of course. Well, not quite: at the end of the commercial, two black kids master the dunk, then a white kid trudges out of the pool, water gushing out of his Nikes. *White boys are gravity-bound dorks. Black men are our hyper-realized selves, our dream selves, our fantasy selves, our selves that can fly.*

Another ubiquitous Nike spot featured Charles Barkley teaching a group of kids at Camp Force how to post up against cows and bulls. When a white kid dribbles the ball off his own foot, Barkley says, "You gonna be rejected by someone who doesn't even have hands"—i.e., a cow. An NBA rookie named Robert "Tractor" Traylor takes the court, and Barkley says, "Show 'em how to do it, Tractor." Tractor maneuvers around a cow and dunks. The commercial ends with a white kid stepping in literal bullshit and Barkley saying, "Uh-oh, Richie, we've got a triple-scooper." *White boys are gravity-bound dorks. Black men are our hyper-realized selves, our dream selves, our fantasy selves, our selves that aren't shitty.*

A third commercial that was omnipresent throughout the Finals was for NBA.com. The Orlando Magic's Penny Hardaway asks various nerdy scientist types—most of whom are wearing glasses and all of whom are wearing white lab coats—to add such features as real-time stats, Java-enabled browsers, and chat rooms to the NBA.com website. Informed that NBA.com already has all these features, he stands up and belligerently asks if NBA.com has the recipe for his mother's meatloaf. Yes, it turns out that NBA.com has that, too. *Black men are physical marvels, but they are only physical marvels. Whenever they attempt to act civilized, they're just pretending; they quickly revert to their simple, animal selves.*

All three of these commercials are saying at least one more thing as well: "It's *our* language in *their* mouths."

FOLLOWING GAME 4, David Robinson spoke to NBC's Ahmad Rashad, after which Bob Costas, NBC's play-by-play sportscaster, said about Robinson, "This is one impressive man. The admirable Admiral." Robinson is poised, dignified, smart, articulate, and it was evident that Costas meant "impressive" in the emotional and intellectual and even spiritual senses as well as in the physical sense (Robinson has Popeye-esque arms). Maybe the color commentator, Doug Collins, was just trying to be a good broadcaster by being vivid, terse, and anecdotal; maybe as an ex-player, the only impressiveness that really registers for him is physical; but in any case, he said, "Bob, I go back to when he [Robinson] was at the Naval Academy and I had the great opportunity to broadcast his games. I'll never forget when they lost in the NCAA tournament to Duke in the Eastern finals. Going in just to say good-bye and say thanks: he was dressed in his whites, the Naval Academy whites, and I'll never forget just the way he looked, how he looked in the uniform. He's quite a man." Costas was caught; he didn't want to be aligned with Collins's panegyric to Robinson's physique, but he would have sounded pathetic if he'd tried to explain what he meant in the first place. It's impossible to overstate the degree to which the broadcast of major spectator sports—football, baseball, and basketball—is shadowed by the homosexual panic implicit in the fact that it consists for the most part of a bunch of out-of-shape white men sitting around talking about black men's buff bodies.

• • •

IMMEDIATELY AFTER San Antonio won the championship, Gregg Popovich, the Spurs' coach and general manager, was interviewed on NBC by Steve Jones. The Spurs' backup shooting guard Jaren Jackson came up behind Popovich, said, "I love you, baby," mussed his hair, and hugged him. It was a genuinely nice moment for a second or two (Popovich hugged him back and said, "I love you, too") until Popovich, fixing his hair, said to Jackson, "Lemme go." As if explaining his behavior, Jackson reiterated, "I love you, baby"—*That's why I was hugging you, man; sorry if I mussed what little hair you've got!* Popovich could tell that Jackson was pouting a little, so he squeezed his arm but then couldn't resist turning back to the camera and saying, "He just wants a contract next year." This line was delivered as if it were nothing more or less than locker-room teasing, but it wasn't that, or at least it wasn't only that, because Jackson, with heartbreaking vulnerability and shamelessness, replied, "I can shoot the apple, baby"—*I'm a good shooter, so please bring me back next season.* A simultaneous lovefest and hardball negotiation conducted, in Kabuki theater, on national television.

FOR ME, THE most concisely symbolic moment in the series occurred during Game 2, when Jess Kersey, a patrician-looking man who must be the oldest ref in the league, said something to Sprewell as he came back onto the court after a time-out. Sprewell apparently couldn't quite hear what Kersey said, so he leaned over and leaned down until his ear was near Kersey's mouth. Kersey repeated whatever it was he had to say. Spree nodded, pointed his two index fingers at him to indicate "I gotcha," then immediately backed away. All the official authority resided in Kersey, but all the unofficial power resided in Sprewell—what a cool gesture those aimed index fingers were. You could feel Kersey trying to connect a little with Sprewell (what he had to say was probably unnecessary) and Sprewell trying to connect a little with Kersey (in the space of two seconds, his eyes melted noticeably). He didn't kowtow to Kersey, but he didn't entirely diss him, either—*What do you want from me, mister? Aiiight, I'll go this far and no farther. I'll meet you here, barely halfway. I'll be funky with you for a sec, but let's not pretend we're tight. Okay, I'm out.*

MYTHS OF PLACE

BLACK/WHITE, EAST/WEST, NORTH/SOUTH, MALE/FEMALE: Group X always needs Group Y to buff its own sense of superiority. It's simple but true: power is a fulcrum. Everybody needs someone to beat up, and the East Coast defines itself as the East Coast by caricaturing the West Coast, which I didn't fully understand until I moved back to the west after growing up in California and living in the East for fifteen years. In this view, the West is—black people are—in a perpetual state of nature. *We are mind-haunted civilization; you are the physical beauty we'll contemplate.*

When Jim Fassel, who was born and raised in California and had coached primarily in the West, was hired to be the head coach of the New York Giants, the *New York Daily News* wondered whether someone who was "accustomed to bikini weather and a pretty passing game would struggle with the elements of player discipline in the He-Man's land of the NFC East."

Boston Celtic Paul Pierce, an all-star, by reputation one of the grittiest players in the NBA, and a native Californian, said, "The hatred for the West Coast player—it's everywhere. Especially in high school. When you go back East, it's always, 'the West is soft.' I can't tell you how many guys I got into it with over that. That probably has something to do with why no one had heard of me until the McDonald's All-American game."

Pierce's then teammate Kenny Anderson, who was born and raised in Queens, told him, "Because there's no ballers on the West Coast like in New York, the mecca of basketball. That's why nobody heard of you."

Kenny Anderson was a high school phenom and a college star but has been an NBA journeyman; inevitably, it's the middle- and lower-rung players who cling to the badge of geographic superiority.

When Larry Bird, longtime Boston Celtic star, was coaching the Indiana Pacers, he said, "The East used to have the defensive powers. But with the new rules, scoring is up, and it hurts us. It's a softer game now, and the West always has had soft teams."

Jalen Rose, then of the Indiana Pacers, viewed it somewhat differently: "The West is about scoring and putting three or four guys out there who can actually put the ball in the basket. In the East, two guys might be robots."

The West is about pretty skills; the East is a manly scrum.

Texas Tech football coach Greg McMackin said, "The West Coast offense is a finesse offense that's built on rhythm. They dink and dunk in the short, quick, passing game so they can have third-and-short situations."

After the Sonics defeated the Knicks in New York several years ago, Seattle's Sam Perkins said, "It's no problem for us being physical. We're not as soft as people say we are. We just don't have the reputation. We're not seen as much on the East Coast. People think we just run and shoot. They don't really see how we are, until today."

New York Yankees pitcher Roger Clemens claims that he's "seen a few times in Anaheim where a guy is throwing a cool game and people get up in the fifth, sixth, or seventh inning and head for the beach."

The myth persists that West Coast fans always arrive late and leave early, whereas East Coast fans supposedly arrive on time and stay until the bitter end: they have true forbearance, persistence, stick-to-itiveness. In actuality, at lopsided games at Yankee Stadium, fans leave in the fifth inning, as they do anywhere else. When the Knicks are way behind, fans throng to the exits midway through the fourth quarter, the same way people do in the rest of the country. When the Yankees were bad during the 1980s, attendance fell dramatically; so, too, at Madison Square Garden, attendance is way down now that the Knicks are terrible.

Philadelphia Phillies manager Larry Bowa, born and raised in Philadelphia, says, "There's more of a sense of urgency to excel on the East Coast. They don't have a lot of other things to do, whereas fans have a lot of stuff to do out there on the West Coast. Going to the ballpark's more laid-back. It's a little more casual. It's really a form of entertainment for them. On the East Coast, it's, 'Hey, we want you to win at all costs. It's our summer. Don't screw it up.' If you're not a mentally tough person and you're traded to an East Coast team, it might have an effect on you—fans calling you a bum. If that bothers you, you might want to get into another line of work. Or try to get traded back out West."

The West is invariably referred to as "out West," as if to underscore that the Northeast is the center of American civilization. China/Japan; Japan/Korea; Athens/Rome; the Roman Empire/Christianity; London/New York; East Coast/West Coast—every society has forever condescended to every society that followed afterward.

In the *New York Review of Books,* Thomas Powers writes, "Larry McMurtry, a widely read and cosmopolitan man despite his reputation as a Western writer . . ."

Jonathan Raban, a British writer who lives in Seattle, says, "Living in the West, I find myself a victim of 'Westism'—that mixture of condescension, sentimentality, and naïve romanticism, which is strangely like old-fashioned sexism. The assumptions of the East about the West—its politics, society, open-air sports like fishing and skiing—are mighty annoying, if you happen to live in a region conceived by New York to be a sort of rugged national park, stretching from the Mississippi to the Pacific, inhabited by unlettered rustics. In actuality, there are many more nerds than Marlboro Men in the West I live in, from Bill Gates to Jeffrey Katzenberg."

A box at the bottom of the front page of the *New York Times* guides readers to stories inside: "G. I. Killed in Afghanistan," "Fujimori Seeks a Comeback," "US Airways Plans Cuts," "Office Shopping Spree," and "Bear Concerns at Yosemite." The West is forever the 22-second nature nonstory at the end of the network news.

Mo Vaughn was raised near Boston and had several good years with the Red Sox before being traded to Anaheim, for whom he was an extremely expensive disappointment. "Being on the West Coast, I learned how much I love the East Coast," he said. "The intensity of the will to succeed just wasn't there. Every place has got its issues. But for me, as a ballplayer, I need to be in the fire. I can't be out there on Mars." Out there. "I've got to be in the mix, man."

Upon being traded to the New York Mets, Vaughn said, "You're in the limelight here and you're going to be seen. If you're not intimidated by it, it can help you as a player. For me, to have that on an everyday basis can only bring your game up, because you can't hide. There's nowhere to go."

This relentless scrutiny was the very thing that drove Vaughn out of Boston—he said he felt suffocated playing in the same place where he had grown up—and in New York he's been an even bigger bust than he was in Anaheim.

"I was brought up in a pressure-packed situation in Boston," he said. "Overall, the East Coast is a get-it-done-yesterday type situation, and I seem to thrive on that." In 2002, his first season with New York, he batted .259—his worst average in ten years—while Anaheim won the World Series. In 2003, he hit .190 while playing in just 27 games.

Geographic snobbery is the last refuge of the fallen.

One of the least motivated players ever to play in the NBA, Benoit Benjamin, shortly after being traded from Seattle to New Jersey, said, "As far as I'm concerned, the real basketball games are on the East Coast."

In a letter to the editor in the December 2002 issue of *Harper's,* Joe Ferullo, of Studio City, California, said, "Mark Slouka rightly argues that September 11 generated an apocalyptic response because Americans considered themselves immune to, and protected by God from, such acts. Let me take his argument further. The attacks of 9/11 generated such a response because they took place in New York City. Many of the people Slouka quotes, and nearly all the media reports he mentions, are from New York. The attacks hit them where they live, and the commentators, although they purport to speak for the nation, have for quite some time spoken for a small world confined by the Hudson, East, and Harlem rivers. I strongly suspect that if those horrible events had occurred instead in Los Angeles, the national (that is to say, New York–based) media reaction would have been different. After an appropriate period of respectful silence, the talking heads and newsweeklies would have trotted out timeworn homilies about how Los Angeles had brought this on itself, thinking it could be isolated from the real world in a bubble of sand, sunshine, and mass-produced make-believe. If Seattle had been the target, I imagine national commentators would have ruminated on how this was one more, though extraordinarily painful, step in that city's decline since the irrationally exuberant dot-com days. An attack on, say, Miami would not have been expanded into evidence that evil had returned to the planet, that the entire world had been irrevocably altered, that nothing would ever be the same anywhere."

New York native Gordon Edelstein, for many years the artistic director of the Seattle Repertory Theatre, said, upon becoming artistic director of the Long Wharf Theatre in New Haven, "In Seattle, when the curtain rises on a play, the audience is open, but their tacit agreement is that life is pretty good, it's important to be comfortable, and human beings actually can be healthy. The curtain rises on a New York audience, and everybody agrees we're basically sick and we want redemption and we want a good time, but we're not made uncomfortable by deeply disturbing news about our psyche. In fact, that feels like the truth to us." Of course this feels like the truth to you: you get to control what's agreed upon as truth.

The issue isn't that this E/W dichotomy isn't indicative of real regional differences; it's that the dichotomy gets completely cartoonized and the "greater than" arrow always points to one side of the equation. Larry King once said, "Bums in New York could run a grocery chain in Des Moines." In my experience, people in the West (or, for that matter, the Midwest) are at least as intelligent and driven as people in the East; they just cloak these qualities in a more understated cultural style.

In Thomas Pynchon's *Mason & Dixon,* Reverend Cherrycoke says, "As to journey west, in the same sense of the Sun, is to live, raise children, grow older, and die, carried along by the stream of the day, whilst to turn Eastward is somehow to resist time and age, to work against the Wind, seek ever the dawn, even, as who can say, defy death." "Eastward" here is capitalized; "west" is lowercased.

The East is part of the history of art; the West is the mere muck of life.

The *New Yorker* sponsored a cruise ship going around the world from Los Angeles to Greece; different *New Yorker* contributors entertained passengers on different legs of the journey. On the L.A.–Australia run, all of the *New Yorker* artists on board ship were cartoonists.

S. Bass, of San Francisco, in a recent letter to the *New Yorker,* wrote: "In lauding Manhattan's street grid plan in his review of 'Gotham: A History of New York City to 1898,' Paul Goldberger fails to comment on one invidious urban effect that was unforeseeable when the plan was adopted in 1811: the grid plan's 'equalization' permits motor vehicle traffic to universally intrude on and interfere with pedestrianism, making New York unlike other great cities in the world, where it's relatively easy when walking to find a quiet side street. In deeming the plan brilliant urban planning, Goldberger seems to be confusing New York's 'determined rambunctiousness' with the stress caused by the grid's constant, omnipresent crush of traffic." New York's much vaunted "energy," in other words, is just gridlock.

Early NBA retiree (and famously fragile) Donny Marshall said several years ago, "I feel more comfortable with the East Coast style of basketball. You go to southern California and you see palm trees and beautiful people." Marshall himself is model-handsome. "I remember our trip to New York to play St. John's when I was at UConn. The people weren't beautiful; they were jittery. Everything was so fast. I loved it."

Mark Twain wrote about New York, "There is something about this ceaseless buzz and hurry and bustle that keeps a stranger in a state of unwholesome excitement all the time, and makes him restless and uneasy."

Even Japanese baseball star Hideki Matsui, when he was being courted by several American baseball teams, told Japanese reporters, "I want to go to an East Coast team where there's some pressure to perform." Or, alternatively and interestingly, a "West Coast team if that team can help me develop further as a player." Skills vs. scrum.

Coming from Philadelphia to Phoenix for his first season, Charles Barkley said, "Guys thought I was too mean in [training] camp, but they don't get it. You can't just show up on opening night and say, 'O.K., now we're going to be mean.' I think living in the sun makes these guys soft. John Havlicek [of the Boston Celtics] told me that. In the East, you wake up, you look out, and there's snow on the ground. You start the day pissed off. Out here"—out here—"you wake up, it's beautiful out. You put on the Bermudas and have breakfast on the porch."

During the 2002 season, Washington State University quarterback Jason Gesser played on a severe ankle strain while leading his team to a victory over UCLA and into the Rose Bowl. It was about as courageous an athletic performance as one could hope to see; if he'd been from Pittsburgh, there would have been much discussion of how both his grandfather and father had worked in the coal mines, but Gesser is from Hawaii, so no one knew what to say to mythologize the moment.

A *New York Times* interviewer didn't understand why Albert Brooks didn't find it a compliment to be called the "West Coast Woody Allen." When she asked him what he'd rather be called, he said, "Why do I have to be called something?" She still didn't get it, so he said, "How about 'the living Stanley Kubrick'?"

I knew San Antonio was going to win the 2000 NBA championship when Tim Duncan shrugged and said, "Nice rims."

In the 2001 NBA Finals, the Los Angeles Lakers were expected to defeat the Philadelphia 76ers easily, but Philadelphia won the first game. Afterward, sportscaster Marv Albert said, "Philly was down, 18–5. If this were a series in the West, you'd feel like Philly didn't believe in themselves. But Philly came back." Only people in the East believe in themselves. Only people in the East have heart. Everyone else is a Scarecrow or, perhaps, the Cowardly Lion. Los Angeles won the next four games, but it had nothing to do with heart or character. They were just, boringly, the better team.

When Arizona beat the Yankees in the 2001 World Series, it wasn't perceived to be a fable; the Diamondbacks got lucky in Game 7. When Anaheim beat the Yankees in the 2002 American

League Division Series, New York only happened to be in a batting slump at the wrong time. When Seattle came back from a 2–0 deficit to beat New York in the American League Championship Series in 1995, the Mariners weren't displaying superior fortitude; the Yankees ran out of steam. Ditto Florida's defeat of the Yankees in the 2003 World Series. When an East Coast team, especially a New York team, wins, it's a morality tale about the little engine that could or, contrariwise, the unstoppable forces of capitalism. When a team from somewhere else wins, it's just, shrug, a game. It's not shrouded in mythology. Whoever owns the story tells its meaning.

A LITTLE EURO TRASH-TALK

Six foreign-born players played in the 2003 NBA All-Star Game, and another seven played in the Rookie Challenge, a game matching the best first-year and second-year players. The game was televised to 212 countries in 41 languages. Of the 430 players in the NBA, 71 are foreign-born, there is at least one player from every continent except Australia, and 26 of the 29 teams have at least one non-American player. New York Knicks coach Lenny Wilkens, who has won (and lost) more games than any coach in NBA history, says, "I wouldn't be surprised if there are double the number of players now in the next five or so years." Seven European players were drafted in the first round of the 2003 NBA draft. Pau Gasol of Spain, now a star with the Memphis Grizzlies, was the third player drafted in 2001. Every team in the NBA now has at least one international scout; representatives from fourteen NBA teams attended the recent European Championships in Turkey. Two of the best and most entertaining teams in the NBA, San Antonio and Dallas, have six and five international players, respectively. Dallas owner Mark Cuban says, "We're in great shape if we ever have to play anybody in soccer for a tiebreaker."

The NBA's official website now lists each player's height and weight not only in feet and pounds but also in meters and kilograms; the league is intent upon expanding the game internationally in the next half-dozen years and played two games in Tokyo to open the 2003–2004 season. Mavericks marketing manager, Will Patton, says, "We've always been trying to lay the groundwork [to build a global market for the game]. Now the foreign players are igniting it."

Watching the Dream Team demolish the opposition in the 1992 Olympics, Andrei Kirilenko, from St. Petersburg, believed "that gods played in the NBA." This season he's emerged as the biggest star on the Utah Jazz, averaging about 16 points a game. A dozen years ago, Eastern European players in the NBA, such as sharpshooters Sarunas Marciulionis and Drazen Petrovic, were very much the exception and were tolerated, barely, because they so expertly filled a niche, rather like Japanese pitchers in the major leagues or European field-goal kickers in the NFL. Foreign players were once perceived to be mechanical and soft, but over the last couple of decades, the game has become Americanized: the '92 Dream Team popularized the sport worldwide; American coaches and players conduct clinics; international teams play exhibitions against U.S. college teams; and Europeans—starting in "kiddie programs," in which they're trained by their countries' top coaches, and then playing professionally from the time they're teenagers—arrive more NBA-ready than their American counterparts. In the 2000 Olympics, the Lithuanian team lost to the U.S. by 2 points; in the 2002 World Championship, the U.S. finished sixth.

Chicago Bulls assistant coach John Bach says, "Like everything American, we have always exported what we do best." Yes, but in a weird sort of parody of the American Dream, an American-born game has been exported and is now being imported back to America, so that, infused with "European craft," it can be re-exported back to the rest of the world. For, as they say on the street, jump shots are for those who can't dunk, and as NBA executive Kim Bohuny says, "Now our teams want international guys. They're seen as fundamentally sound. And they can shoot, where more and more American players can't." Gasol says, "We don't have the athleticism. We don't have the jumping ability or the strength of the American players. But we have more skills." Kirilenko says European players "pay much more attention to shooting in practice, attention to the team game, like learning grammar in school." Yugoslavian coach Marin Sedlacek says, "For so long, the NBA game has been one-on-one street ball, or maybe pick-and-roll." Tony Parker, Jr., age 21, is starting and starring at point guard for the San Antonio Spurs; Tony Parker, Sr., who played college basketball in the U.S. and professionally in Europe, says, "Tony comes out of that very structured European type of basketball, especially in France. It's cerebral basketball. They like to run a lot of set plays over there, and that's the only basketball Tony knows. He's very rarely gotten a chance to play open, free playground ball. He's mature and poised and doesn't know about being selfish, because the European game is the open man gets the shot. They stay in the flow of the game, respect the coach, respect your teammate, and respect your adversaries." Hear the implicit criticism of the homeys? Parker's San Antonio coach, Gregg Popovich, praises Parker's "great demeanor" and "high intelligence."

George Karl, a frequent critic of NBA players' work habits, and the coach of the U.S. team that was badly outplayed by Spain, Yugoslavia, and Argentina in the World Championship, says, "Over the past four or five years, the young European is out-dueling the American youngster. They may have better fundamentals, be more serious, more committed when they come to the NBA. It's their passion to play here, while some of our kids may feel we're rewarding them with the NBA. They may not be as professional or as passionate as the European kids coming in. It's their heart and hunger." Former Detroit Pistons coach Chuck Daly says about NBA players, "They better pay attention to what's happening. Those guys that want to get into drugs and chasing young girls and not shooting basketballs better think twice if they want to make it to the NBA, because somebody wants their jobs. [European players] are willing to practice many, many hours on shooting. Our people are not. We have great athletes who don't have the skill of shooting the basketball."

Indiana guard Jamaal Tinsley, echoing Daly, says, "These guys are going after our jobs. This isn't just an American thing anymore." Minnesota's all-star forward Kevin Garnett says, "I think it's two different styles of play. I think we're a lot more athletic. Basketball's not as big overseas. So I think they tend to cling on mechanics and fundamentals, while we as Americans are exposed to many different parts of the game. I just think we have a lot more exposure as far as bringing new dimensions to the game." Retired guard Dell Curry says, "I can't explain it, but the Ameri-

can point guards seem to be able to understand the game better."
Kenny Smith, a former NBA player who is now a commentator
for TNT, at the 2001 draft wondered why so many teams were
taking foreign players rather than "known quantities."

The NBA players sound a tad defensive, as well they might,
for the NBA is Reparation Theatre—a photo negative of American race relations—a place where strong, young black men have
some of the power, much of the money, and all of the fun—and
the European players represent the correction of the correction, a
rescue mission back to the past.

BEING ICHIRO

I agonized all spring 2001 about whether to get cable TV. I didn't want my 8-year-old daughter, Natalie, to get hooked on the Cartoon Network, but I wanted to be able to watch the Seattle Mariners, who were off to such a brilliant start—not just winning nearly all of their games but also playing a really new (for them), beautiful brand of team baseball: sacrifice bunts rather than 3-run homers. Twice I called the cable company and scheduled appointments for installation, only to cancel both times.

About a week and a half into the season, I was listening to a Mariners–Oakland A's game on the radio; after a few innings, I couldn't stand it any longer and ran around the corner to a sports bar. Oakland's Terrence Long was on first base. The next batter singled to right field, and when Long tried to run from first to third base (a relatively routine maneuver), the Mariners' right fielder, number 51, Ichiro Suzuki—the first Japanese position player in the major leagues and a star who, like Madonna or Cher or Pelé, goes only by his first name—threw a line drive from medium-deep right field all the way to the third baseman, who easily tagged out Long.

The bar erupted, the announcer went berserk, I got that weird tingle down my spine I get about twice a decade, and for the next twenty-four hours, pretty much all anyone in Seattle could talk about was The Throw. Several players, coaches, and broadcasters said it was the single greatest throw they'd ever seen. "The ball came out of a cannon; it was quick and powerful." "An eye-high laser." "It was like something out of *Star Wars*." Even Terrence Long agreed: "It was going to take a perfect throw to get me, and it was a perfect throw."

Asked to explain how he was able to throw the runner out, Ichiro said, through his translator: "The ball was hit right to me. Why did he run when I was going to throw him out?"

Cable was installed by the end of the week.

A COUPLE OF months later, the Mariners were again playing the A's, this time in Seattle. In the bottom of the sixth inning, with the score tied and runners on first and third with one out, Ichiro came up to bat. He took the first pitch from Mark Mulder for a strike, the next pitch for a ball, fouled off the next pitch, fouled off another couple of pitches, then calmly lined the next pitch just over the outstretched glove of the shortstop and into left field for a single, scoring the runner from third and putting the Mariners ahead for good, 4–3.

Bill Krueger, a former Mariners pitcher who now does postgame analysis for Fox Sports Northwest, said to me, "I thought Mulder went at Ichiro perfectly. He went away with a fast ball, came inside off the plate, and also came inside twice. Ichiro fouled off every one of those pitches. With two strikes, he threw him another fast ball away that, I swear, he hit right out of the catcher's glove. It's almost like he's playing pepper—it's just this little game he's playing—but this isn't a little game. The game is played by men that want to beat you bad, and they're very talented, and Ichiro doesn't know the guys he's facing. I find that incredible."

Center fielder Mike Cameron said about Ichiro: "He puts the ball basically where he wants it. I mean, the shortstop will shift over to the left side of the field a little bit, and Ichi will hit it right where the guy just took two steps from."

Former major leaguer George Arias, a teammate of Ichiro's in Japan, said about him, "He's got such hand-eye coordination, it's like he's playing wiffleball out there."

Ichiro, said Japanese broadcaster Kazuo Ito, is a "genius with a bat."

ICHIRO, WHO IS 30 years old, stands 5'9", weighs 160 pounds, throws right, and bats left, was regarded as the best player in Japan and perhaps the best hitter in the history of Japanese baseball, where he won seven consecutive batting titles and seven Gold Glove awards and was chosen for seven consecutive all-star games. In a recent poll, he was judged to be the most recognizable person in Japan. (The emperor came in a distant second.)

The Mariners paid the Orix BlueWave $13.1 million for the right to negotiate with Ichiro, and in 2000 he signed a three-year, $14 million contract, becoming the first nonpitcher from Japan to play in the major leagues. Ichiro was the first rookie ever to draw the most votes for the All-Star Game (3,373,035). The first three months of the season, he led the American League in hitting, with an average almost always at or above .350. However, during the week before the All-Star Game and for a couple of weeks after, Ichiro struggled, at one point going 0 for 18. The second half of the season was a crucial test: Could he adjust to the adjustments that other teams had made to his game? From August 3 to August 24, Ichiro went on a 21-game hitting streak, during which he hit for a .451 average, scored 17 runs, and hit .708 with runners in scoring position. Ichiro wound up winning the American League Most Valuable Player Award, the Rookie of the Year Award, and a Gold Glove Award, leading the league in batting average (.350), hits (242), and stolen bases (56), and coming in second in runs scored (127). The Mariners won 116 games during the regular season, tying for the most wins ever and winning the division by 14 games, although they lost the American League Championship Series, 4–1, to the Yankees, who expertly exploited Ichiro's one apparent weakness—his tendency to swing at pitches out of the strike zone rather than accept a base-on-balls. In 2002 Ichiro walked more than twice as many times as he had in 2001, but he had 34 fewer hits, 18 fewer RBIs, 25 fewer stolen bases, and he batted "only" .321. The Mariners didn't make the playoffs, but Ichiro again started for the American League All-Star Team and again received a Gold Glove Award as the best defensive right-fielder in the American League. In 2003, Ichiro and the Mariners had a similar, close-but-no-cigar year, Ichiro slumping badly in the last half of the season, as he did in 2002, though he still wound up hitting .312.

AT THE BEGINNING of each game, when Ichiro runs to his position in right field, he runs quite hard, much harder than any of the other Mariners, a near sprint, and when he arrives at his spot, he gives a quick, short wave with his glove to the fans in the right-field stands. This wave is both a greeting and a dismissal—the last direct interaction he'll have with fans for the rest of the game and, in its mixture of respectfulness and artful evasion, an utterly characteristic gesture. God, as they say, doesn't return phone calls.

At every game, throughout Safeco Field in Seattle but especially along the right-field foul line and in the right-field bleachers (now known as Area 51—"where baseballs disappear"), there are hundreds upon hundreds of kids and adults, Japanese and Japanese-Americans and other Asian-Americans, all going what has come to be known as "Ichigaga." They wear number-51 jerseys and blue baseball hats with "water warrior" (i.e., mariner) in kanji and hold up Japanese flags and signs, some in English but many in Japanese, saying things like "Ichi-Hero," "We Love Ichiro," "#51 Get a Hit," and, my favorite, "Ichi-ro Heart Out, A-Rod and Junior."

This last one perfectly captures the current Seattle zeitgeist: good riddance to stats-obsessed behemoths Alex Rodriguez, Ken Griffey, Jr., and Boeing; nervous optimism about the continued health of Microsoft and Amazon; and a rapturous embrace of Ichiro's Pacific Rim virtues (modesty and understatement masking a fierce devotion to precision and success). The person Ichiro replaced in right field, Jay Buhner—a Texan who has a shaved head and is nicknamed Bone, the team prankster and rah-rah guy who tended either to hit a home run or strike out and who after being injured virtually the entire year retired at the end of the 2001 season—is the perfect embodiment of the past: the Olds Cutlass that the Honda replaced. One night, a fan in Area 51 rather forlornly held up a sign saying, "We miss you, Bone."

ASKED TO POSE for the cover of *Sports Illustrated* at the end of the first month of his first season, Ichiro declined, saying, "I haven't done anything yet." Told that his 19-game hitting streak tied for the season's best in the American League and asked for his reaction, he said, "I wouldn't have known if you didn't tell me." In a game against Kansas City in May, Ichiro reached high above the wall, caught what otherwise would have been a home run, fell to the ground, did a backward somersault, adjusted his sunglasses, and then slowly pulled the ball out from his glove to show that he had caught it. Asked to analyze the play, he said, "It was a fly ball; I caught it."

The first two months of the season, I was struck over and over by this discrepancy: Ichiro would perform some extraordinary feat on the field and then, when asked about it, would inevitably question the interviewer's premise or flatten out the praise. Against the bottomless hype and megalomania of contemporary American sports, Ichiro's strut-free sanity seemed strange and new.

IN 2001 A COMMERCIAL in Japanese for Consolidated Restaurants played on mainstream English-language radio stations in

Seattle. A Washington Mutual billboard near Safeco Field welcomed the all-stars in Japanese. The Pacific Plaza shopping center printed 30,000 brochures, in Japanese and English, promoting special offers at its stores and restaurants. A large number of restaurants printed menus in kanji. At the Mariners' team stores, Japanese-speaking employees are always on hand, there are more than a hundred copies of a book in Japanese about major-league baseball, and number 51 is by far the best-selling jersey. At Safeco—majority-owned, as the Mariners are, by Hiroshi Yamauchi, the president of Nintendo—a rotating billboard behind home plate advertises Nintendo's Game Boy Advance, sales of Asian foods at the ballpark's Intentional Wok and Bullpen Bento have increased by 30 percent, all of the signs in the media elevators are in Japanese as well as English, and nearly a quarter of the press box is given over to Japanese reporters. Safeco has been specially wired so that all Mariners home games can be televised live in HDTV on the national NHK network in Japan, where workers jostle one another for the best spot at lunch counters to watch Mariners games, taxi drivers keep radios tuned to play-by-play broadcasts from Safeco, and sports reports have a "major league corner" with U.S. results. The "Ichiro tour" (round-trip flight from Tokyo to Seattle, two games, three nights in a hotel) costs as much as $1,700 per person. Ichiro, the generator of all this activity and the object of all this attention, said, "I think the Japanese people are very much swayed by whatever is popular at the time. A few years ago, the Olympics was in Japan and everyone was into the Olympics."

ICHIRO AND HIS wife, Yumiko Fukushima, a former Japanese television broadcaster, live in a Seattle suburb. Ichiro reportedly watches little television and few movies, doesn't use a computer, during the baseball season doesn't play golf (though he loves the game), and doesn't drink. Instead, he plays Go, collects coins, calls friends in Japan, grows bonsai. A Japanese magazine once asked him why he had the hobbies of an old fogy. He does seem to have an old soul.

While other players in the dugout spit out sunflower seeds or talk or clap or pace, Ichiro studies his black, lacquered bat, spinning it, rubbing it. Before the game, he carefully knocks the mud out of his spikes with a piece of wood; other players tend to let the equipment manager handle such duties.

Asked once, by a Japanese journalist, what he wanted for a gift, he said, "A car-washing set." When he was younger, he would clean his apartment three times a day. "It probably sounds fishy," he said, "but when I clean, my heart and mind become clean."

Before every pitch during every at-bat, he swings the bat over his head clockwise, points his right arm directly at the pitcher, stretches his left arm, bends his elbow to touch his right shoulder and tug on his uniform, holds that position, and then releases and cocks the bat to hit. While he's doing this, the world seems to stop momentarily, and we seem to be going back in time to—or is this only my very Western projection?—some ancient purification rite.

YUKI SATO, a Japanese woman who now lives in Seattle, said about Ichiro: "You can tell he really likes baseball because he expresses all of his passion but doesn't show it. He's a human being that has a lot of emotion, just doesn't show the emotion on the face. In here." She pointed to her heart. "You can feel his emotions, anyway. Japanese traditionally don't want to cry or be angry, don't want to show people how you're feeling. Particularly men don't show how they feel."

Hiroshi Tanaka, the tour guide of an Ichiro tour, said, "We call it a blue flame. A blue flame is hotter than red, but it doesn't show itself. Ichiro has a fighting spirit, but it's inner. Outside, it's calm. Like a candle."

This seems to me an utterly persuasive and un-American idea: it's not his fist-pumping that makes us feel something; it's his absence of fist-pumping. By not displaying his emotions, he allows fans to feel the emotions more deeply. A former student of mine, who's Chinese, once explained to me that in Asian culture the less one shows one's feelings, the more one is expressing one's personality.

IN JULY 2001, in a game against the Giants, in the sixth inning, Ichiro lifted a lazy fly ball to right field that was virtually certain to be caught. He ran hard, but not so hard that other players would accuse him of grandstanding. It's a subtle cultural transaction, it seems to me: his whole game is predicated on outhustling the opposition, but he can't hustle so hard that the other players regard him as Goody Two Shoes—the kid who studies so overzealously for the exam that he's practically co-teaching the course. He wants the other players to like him, which they do, precisely because he's alert to nuances like these. He's that rare thing: the class genius who isn't a nerd.

ASKED WHAT HE'D miss about Japanese baseball, Ichiro said, "There is nothing I will miss about Japanese baseball. Off the field, I will miss my dog." Asked to confirm a rumor that a Japanese magazine was offering $1 million for a nude photo of him, Ichiro said, "If that was true, I'd take the picture myself and send it in." Asked how much they'd have to pay him to pose nude, he said, "I'd do it if they'd disappear." You mean, he was asked, you'd do it if they'd stop following you? "I'd do it if they'd disappear from the planet," he replied.

Ichiro wears Oakley sunglasses (the ultrachic Juliet model). Nobuyoshi Tsubota, the master craftsman who makes three hand-crafted gloves a year for Ichiro, said he makes Ichiro's gloves particularly large and flexible because "he likes to make the behind-the-back catch." Told once that he looks like Brad Pitt—both are small and have facial hair (Ichiro has long sideburns, a goatee, and a thin mustache)—Ichiro said, "It feels like going up to the heavens. I want to fly." Asked what he would like to do on a day off, Ichiro said, "I want to watch American kids playing baseball on a grass field, running around, and getting hoarse in the voice with my wife." A recent Japanese publication alludes to a moment when Ichiro, "in an outrageous get-up with a shaved head and gold-capped teeth, smashed a beer bottle on someone's head while crying out 'rap-group.'" Asked to reveal the name of his dog, Ichiro declined, saying, "I do not have the dog's permission."

He seems to be both wise man and wise guy, the embodiment of both traditional Japanese culture and the reaction against it.

BEFORE EVERY GAME, while Ichiro stretches, throws, and catches, then takes batting practice and, later, does running drills, a dozen Japanese cameramen set up their tripods just past the Mariners' dugout along the right-field foul line and aim their lenses only at him (not, for instance, at Kazuhiro Sasaki, the Mariners' all-star relief pitcher), and another couple of dozen Japanese reporters are on the field or in the press box, chronicling or attempting to chronicle every single thing he does, including what he ate for dessert.

Once, when he was seen eating a Drumstick ice cream cone, a Japanese reporter asked one of Ichiro's interpreters, "Does it have nuts?"

The Ichiro Rules, in place since spring training of his first year, stipulate that he doesn't talk before games, and after games only when he's in the mood (in the case of the Japanese press, only to Keizo Konishi of the Kyodo News Service, the pool reporter for the entire Japanese contingent), and no TV cameras are allowed near his locker.

Konishi says, "Ichiro's a good guy, but in his personality he's a cautious guy. The situation with the Japanese press can be uncomfortable. We have to look for information about him every day, but in the U.S. he is part of a team and he isn't always the key player in the game every day."

In a statement in mid-July 2001, Ichiro said that because of several recent off-the-field encounters with members of the Japanese media, he'd no longer talk to any Japanese journalists. While the ban was in effect, Ichiro went into a brief slump. The ban was lifted after five days; maybe a fishbowl existence, for all he complains about it, is one of the useful tensions of his life, and without it he doesn't know how to be.

HALFWAY THROUGH his first season, after numerous entreaties, I was finally granted, to the consternation of several Japanese reporters, an interview with Ichiro; they'd been pursuing their subject for months if not years. I was the object of much envy. And yet, what had I been granted access to? Less an interview than a simulation of an interview. The moment it began, Ichiro turned his chair away from me, as he does with every interviewer, so that he was facing his locker and his back was to me. When I asked him why he did this, he said, "I cannot show my face—the face in my house—to the public, because I don't want the public to see it. At the same time, I cannot show my face on the field in my house." He said through his translator that the interview would last exactly ten minutes; Ichiro would check the clock and inform me when my time was up. Sitting next to him, I was struck, mainly, by how incongruously muscular his legs are compared to the rest of his small, compact body; he can leg-press 360 pounds.

"Do you think it's fair to say that part of you is a very traditional Japanese man and part of you is a modern Japanese man?" I asked. "And if so, do you think that's why Japanese fans are so fascinated by you—because they feel the same contradiction with themselves?"

He said, "First of all, I don't know what a traditional Japanese is and what a modern Japanese is." He asked me to define my terms, which I attempted to do. He didn't automatically enter the terrain of the question; he maintained his distance toward the discourse; most athletes, most people, don't do that. This detachment is connected, of course, to his ability to concentrate during the game. He sat in silence and thought for maybe a minute. "It's very difficult to answer," he finally said.

When I asked him whether he would rather not answer, he said, "It's not that I'd rather not answer; it's just that I'm thinking how to answer."

He genuinely seemed to want to bear down on the question, contemplate it, worry it, rather than just process it through a cliché machine. Finally, he said, "For instance, maybe people call me traditional because I take care of my gloves and bat very well."

I asked him if he regarded his equipment as "spiritual." He said, "Mucho. Mucho. Other players look at their equipment differently. This is not only baseball equipment to me, but they are part of me. You know, parts of my body."

Almost without exception, other players identified his extraordinary hand-eye coordination as the ability that sets him apart; when I asked him how he developed this, he said, "I haven't had any special practice for hand-eye coordination. It's ongoing every day."

When I asked him whether he thought fans responded so powerfully to him in part because of the evident care with which he performs his tasks, he predictably deflected the question, saying, "I don't know whether my style is different from other players. Sometimes I may be casual. Sometimes I may be very careful. I don't know what makes fans attracted to me. I don't know; you tell me."

Asked why he always deflects praise, he said, "After I make a good play, there's the next thing coming up right away. I cannot be praised all the time. You have to keep going. If my one play finishes the game, that's different. Don't get me wrong; I always appreciate the fans and the media mentioning to me my good play. Maybe when I go to bed, I can think of that good play. But the next day, a new day, I would not carry it with me."

I asked him how, with all the attention paid to him, he maintains his modesty. He said, "Whenever I accomplished something in Japan, they praised me more than they should. And when I didn't accomplish something, they looked down on me more than they should. So I cannot be influenced by 'overrated' or 'underrated'—that's what I learned playing seven years in Japan."

Demurral, denial, deflection, self-confidence, go figure it out yourself, generosity, stay in the moment—the full repertoire of Ichiro batting techniques. The interview lasted nearly three times longer than was originally allotted. A few Japanese reporters expressed surprise at how much time I'd been granted with him, but I was no closer to penetrating the mystery than they were.

AFTER A MARINERS loss toward the end of June in that first season of his in America, I asked his translator, Hide Sueyoshi, for a single image that, to him, embodied Ichiro. Sueyoshi thought about this for a while and finally said, with a shrug, "Maybe just him over there in his street clothes. That's just the picture of him I see in my mind. Off-season, him just wearing loose jeans and clothing."

I had no idea what he was talking about, but I turned around and looked. There was Ichiro, heading out the door into the perfect summer night in his fashionable but casual dark shoes and pants and shirt and new nonspiky haircut, carrying a backpack and speaking with calm animation into his cell phone. He seemed to be just an ordinary young man who happens to have been, as Mariners utility player Mark McLemore said, "blessed with the ability to play baseball better than most people."

"Celebrity," John Updike wrote, "is a mask that eats into the face," and I could feel, looking at Ichiro, how fiercely he doesn't want his face to be eaten. Asked before the season whether he felt anxiety about moving to America, he said, "I still can't speak

English, and there's a lot of pressure. There are a lot of things I worry about, unexpected things, because the mentality and manners are different. Even if there are things that become stressful, I think they're interesting. Isn't it because of those things that I am able to be struck by the significance of being alive?" He's just trying to stay in the groove and not stop being struck by the significance. The moment the mask is in place, he smashes it.

When I told my daughter that I was writing about Ichiro, she wondered aloud if she might be able to meet him, then reconsidered: "I wouldn't want to get him dirty." Ted Heid, the Mariners' Pacific Rim coordinator and an occasional translator for Ichiro, compared Ichiro's iconic status in Japan with Madonna's or Elvis's in the West. His nickname in Japan is, in fact, Elvis. Ichiro, Madonna, Elvis: each of them is somehow, simultaneously, impossibly, an avatar of both absolute conformity and absolute rebellion. We invent idols that contain the contradictions within ourselves.

During the middle of the 2001 baseball season, on Beacon Hill in Seattle, at Blaine Memorial United Methodist, a nearly 100-year-old Japanese-American church, the Reverend Eugene Hall asked the congregation, "Who is it we turn to for all of our hopes and blessings?" Most people mumbled the expected response: "Jesus." A college student shouted out: "Ichiro!" The congregation went wild.

MATSUI AMONG THE AMERICANS

HIDEKI MATSUI IS THE ANTI-ICHIRO: TALL AND MUSCULAR, not small and wiry; home runs instead of singles; earnest rather than witty. Where Ichiro is a dizzying mix of contrary and contradictory attitudes toward Japanese society, Matsui embodies its most traditional aspects. During the U.S. stars' tour of Japan in the fall of 2002, Ichiro, asked a question by a Japanese reporter, answered, of course, in Japanese. The Yankees' Jason Giambi interrupted him: "Hey, you've got to speak English now. You're a big-leaguer." Ichiro said, "Shut up, dude." When Matsui lost a home-run hitting contest to Barry Bonds during the same tour, Matsui said, "Well, at least I had five homers, and eight-to-five looks pretty good to me. He gave me advice and also coached me to close my shoulder. Today became a memorable day for me. I really admire his power, and he sure is the number-one hitter in the world." Asked if he thought Matsui would achieve success in the major leagues, Ichiro characteristically deconstructed the question: "'Success' is such a vague word. The records, numbers, and opinions of other people are secondary. I never set personal statistical goals." At his debut press conference in New York, Matsui, asked if he thought he could duplicate his 2002 year in Japan (50 home runs, 107 RBIs, .337 batting average) in 2003 with the Yankees, said, "It's probably going to be a little difficult, but I will try really hard to see if I can get results close to what I had last year. My strongest point is that I can hit home runs, and I hope I can produce the same result in America."

MATSUI AND THE Yankees are a perfect fit. Clean-cut, pleasant, old-school, bromide-bound, Matsui and many of the Yankee stars (Derek Jeter, Mariano Rivera, Bernie Williams, Joe Torre, Mike Mussina), inevitably described as "classy" or a "class act," have configured public personae so bland and all-encompassing that anything remotely real rarely penetrates or escapes the heat shields they've erected.

Jean Afterman, the Yankees' assistant general manager, who was instrumental in brokering the deal ($21 million for three years) that brought Matsui to the Bronx, says, "He played for the functional equivalent of the Yankees of Japan [the Yomiuri Giants], the most popular team in the biggest city, and he was the star." The Yomiuri Giants established the game in Japan, are one of the very few profitable franchises in Japanese baseball, are the only team whose every game is broadcast on nationwide network television, and are owned by Japan's largest media conglomerate (the owner of the Giants also owns the world's largest newspaper, *Yomiuri Shimbun,* with a daily circulation of ten million). From the time Matsui became a free agent at the end of 2002, he wanted to play for the Yankees, and he reportedly told his agent, Arn Tellem, who is also Giambi's agent, to get a deal done with them.

While the Yankees pursued Matsui, they formed a marketing alliance with the Giants: they'll share facilities and learn about each other's training methods and front-office operations, the Yankees will help the Giants scout in Latin America while the Giants will help the Yankees scout in Asia, and the Yankees' television network, YES, agreed to broadcast some Giants games. The teams will also exchange minor-league personnel, including coaches. When confronted with allegations that this informal agreement included a sub rosa understanding that Matsui would negotiate only with the Yankees and that the contract would include hidden income for Matsui that would allow the Yankees to circumvent a portion of the luxury tax, the Yankees—with the honesty for which their owner, George Steinbrenner, is renowned—claimed that their new association wouldn't give them an edge in negotiations with Matsui. Rob Manfred, executive vice president of Major League Baseball, said, apparently with a straight face, "Based on what we know on how the negotiations went, we see nothing preordained in Matsui going to the Yankees."

BORN IN 1974, Matsui grew up in Kanazawa, Ishikawa. As a boy, he hit the ball so far right-handed that his older brother forced him to hit left-handed in pickup games. (He still bats left but throws right.) Much bigger than his classmates, he used his size to defend his friends from bullies. He became a national legend when, in the Koshien high school tournament, he was intentionally walked five times; while fans booed and yelled and some even threw garbage on the field (virtually unheard of in Japan), he quietly dropped his helmet and ran to first base each time without complaining. Ted Heid, a Pacific Rim scout, says, "Matsui is a stoic kid, with great character. He's not only deeply religious but generous and very close to his family." Until leaving for the U.S. in February for his first spring training (followed by 150 members of the Japanese media, who chartered their own flight to New York), he lived in an exclusive Tokyo apartment tower, and he keeps to himself and is single—"the cost of being so focused," one publication speculated.

Matsui acquired the nickname "Godzilla" in high school, according to Ken Marantz, a *Daily Yomiuri* writer: "At the Koshien tournament, Matsui would grit his teeth as he was swinging. One reporter said he looked like Godzilla because his teeth were all in line. At the time, one of the large animation Godzilla puppets had been stolen. A reporter wrote that it showed up at Koshien Stadium." Matsui claims to "like the nickname a lot. Godzilla is a very strong creature but also has a good heart, and my face looks kind of like Godzilla. My face is scary." His former coach says his face is "tough, almost rather ugly," and a recent international edition of *Newsweek* compared his pockmarked face to "a big, unpeeled potato."

He's variously described as "a straight arrow," "a loner," "shy," "kind of an introvert"; his friend Kazumi Oshiro says, "He doesn't make any close friends." He's 6'2", 210 pounds—huge by Japanese standards—and there's something of the apologetic giant about him. Kiyoshi Nakahata, his former hitting coach, says, "In games he's not bold. He's so kind that his kindness doesn't mesh well with the game." There's also something deeply forlorn about Hideki Matsui: the self-imposed isolation of the obsessive hero. Prometheus chained to home plate.

• • •

HE PLAYED IN 1,250 consecutive games—the second-longest streak in the history of Japanese baseball.

In 2002, his last season in Japan, he led the Central League in walks, on-base percentage, average, home runs, and slugging percentage.

He's won home run and RBI titles three times each, has been the league MVP three times, has led his team to four Japan Series.

His career totals in Japan—901 runs, 1,290 hits, 332 home runs, 889 RBIs, .304 average—are better than Ichiro's in every category except batting average, although Warren Cromartie, who has played in both the major leagues and in Japan, says Matsui's only "an average fielder with an average arm." One scout called him "defensively a nonentity" (he played center field in Japan but plays left field for New York). He also has average speed and is an average base runner.

He wears number 55 in honor of Sadaharu Oh's one-season home-run record.

He's stats-obsessed.

WHEN MATSUI HELD a press conference to announce that he was leaving Japanese baseball, he wrote his talking points in pen on his hand and he had tears in his eyes. Legendary Japanese player and former Giants manager Shigeo Nagashima told him "a number of times to continue playing for the Giants," Matsui says, "and it was very difficult for me to tell him of my decision. For the past year, I played with the Giants, and that meant I couldn't share my dream with my teammates or the fans. I had to avoid thinking about it by making every effort to place a lid on my selfishness. I wouldn't have worried about the decision if I weren't the cleanup batter for the Giants." Matsui "agonized over it to the end. I tried to tell myself I needed to stay here for the prosperity of Japanese baseball, but my personal desire to go over there and play didn't go away. In the end I decided to go with what my gut said. This is the first time I've ever been faithful to myself. My greatest regret is what the fans will think. Some might call me a traitor. Once over there, I will do my best, as if my life were on the line, so the fans will be glad I went. The only thing I can say is, 'I am sorry.'"

Asked, at the beginning of his first MLB season, if he had any regrets about leaving Japan to play in the United States, Ichiro said, "I have no regrets following my dream to play in the major leagues. In fact, my only regret would have been if I didn't follow my dream." Upon arriving in the U.S., Ichiro said, "Hey, Seattle, wassup?"

ICHIRO SAYS, "I don't play baseball for other people; I play baseball for myself." When asked if he had any special feelings after playing his first spring-training game with the Mariners, Ichiro said, "Today was just another game to me. I know it has some importance to the media, but not to me. Even being the first game, I was excited, not anxious." Matsui, on the other hand, tends to press under pressure, because baseball is everything to him. During the U.S. all-stars' 2002 tour of Japan, which Japanese fans hoped would showcase Matsui's home-run prowess— every time he came to bat, the public-address system played "We Are the Champions"—he hit no home runs and went 5-for-31 in the seven-game series. With each failure, his shoulders slumped lower, and he gripped the bat handle more tightly. In the bottom of the ninth inning of the tie-breaking seventh game, with Japan behind 4–2 and the bases loaded, Matsui, with a chance to redeem himself, weakly grounded out to end the game and the series. So, too, during his home-run duel with Barry Bonds before one of the games, he was so anxious that Bonds came over and massaged his shoulders, trying to get him to relax a little.

U.S. manager Art Howe said about Matsui, "I think he might have been trying a little too hard in this series."

His own manager, Tatsunori Hara, said, "I think he was a bit tight. He probably played only at about twenty percent of his potential."

Matsui himself said, "During this series, I found out there are a lot of things I need to work on. I just have to accept the result and try hard when I get to America so I can show what I can do. I want to put the lessons I learned in this season to good use next year. I have to show the fans a bigger Matsui. Otherwise, there's no point in my going over there." More so than most players, certainly in the U.S. and even those in Japan, he's aware of fans' fantasies of him, and he badly wants to live up to these fantasies—which makes him seem quite likable but also enormously vulnerable and somewhat naïve. And, indeed, he didn't quite live up to the hype in his first year, with a merely good .287 average and 16 home runs.

RANDY LEVINE, the president of the New York Yankees, said, at the beginning of the January 2003 press conference at the Marriott Marquis that introduced Matsui as a Yankee, "Today, as we stand at Times Square, the crossroads of the world, in New York, the capital of the world, we once again demonstrate that Yankee Stadium is the baseball capital of the world."

"Two hours before the press conference began," Yankees announcer Charlie Steiner said, "the room was packed"—with 500 journalists. "That gives you some idea of the enormity of the signing of Hideki Matsui, and what it means in terms of the Yankees as a worldwide brand."

Four television stations carried the press conference live in Japan, where it was two in the morning. To accommodate more than fifty Japanese reporters, the Yankees set up a special tent for Matsui press conferences during spring training and an auxiliary locker room during the season.

At the press conference, Matsui, sounding as if he were reading from a teleprompter, said, over and over, "I'll try my best. I'll work hard. I'll do my best." He also said: "I'm really honored to be able to come to this beautiful city. . . . Today has been one of the happiest days of my life. . . . I'd like to try as hard as possible to become one of the team members of the New York Yankees and to be accepted in the city. . . . I can't wait to stand in the batter's box at Yankee Stadium, where honorable and very famous players have stepped. The ideal ballplayer is Babe Ruth. I want to be that kind of ballplayer, to give back to the baseball fans. I want to stand in the same batter's box where Babe Ruth and Lou Gehrig stood. I'll try really hard to bring a World Series championship to this city."

George Steinbrenner—who recently said, "I used to be an isolationist, but now I see the benefits of reaching out worldwide"—said about Matsui at the end of the media session, "What a nice young man." Yankee triumphalism had another willing convert.

BRING THE PAIN

Pain is just weakness leaving your body.

—SLOGAN OF THE JOHNS HOPKINS
UNIVERSITY CREW TEAM

WINNERS, THOUGH—THE YANKEES, MICHAEL JORDAN, TIGER Woods, et al.—bore me silly; there's nothing compelling to me about them, because there's so little of the human predicament in their shiny glory. My former writing teacher, the novelist John Hawkes, often used to say, "Failure is the only subject."

During the 1998 and 1999 baseball seasons, while he was being sued for divorce, Atlanta Braves relief pitcher Mark Wohlers had difficulty getting the ball anywhere near the plate. In '98, his earned-run-average (ERA) was 10.00, which is terrible; in '99 it was 27.00, which is unheard-of awful. "I convinced myself the reason I couldn't pitch straight was because I blew out my elbow," Wohlers said, "even though deep down I don't know what it was. The mind is a powerful thing."

Karl Newell, a kinesiologist at the University of Illinois, says, "Consciousness gets in the way. If a pianist starts worrying where his fingers go while he's playing, it will change the performance."

Atlanta Braves catcher Dale Murphy made a few bad throws to second base during a spring-training game in 1977. The next day, when an opponent tried to steal second base, Murphy threw the ball to the outfield fence on one hop. Later that year he twice hit his own pitcher in the back on throws to second base. "Your mind won't let your natural abilities flow," he said. "Your mind interferes, and you start thinking, 'Where am I throwing? What am I doing?' instead of just throwing. Your mind starts working against you." Unable even to return the ball to the pitcher, he was forced to move to the outfield, where he became a perennial all-star.

At age 19, Steve Gasser was one of the stars of the Minnesota Twins' minor-league system. In 1988, having been traded to the New York Mets and pitching in Class A ball, he walked 11 batters and threw 7 wild pitches in one inning, walked 21 batters and threw 13 wild pitches in 6 innings. He never pitched again.

Allan Lans, the Mets' psychiatrist, says, "Everybody brings their personality to the game. It all comes down to an anxiety response. In baseball, people talk about someone getting wild. Then everyone comes rushing to the rescue to fix it and they just make the problem worse. 'Just throw the damn ball,' I tell them. 'Stop thinking too much.'"

In *I of the Vortex: From Neurons to Self,* Rodolfo Llinás writes, "That which we call thinking is the evolutionary internalization of movement."

Science writer Brian Hayes agrees: "Only organisms that move have brains. A tree has no need of a central nervous system because it's not going anywhere, but an animal on the prowl needs to see where it's headed and needs to predict, even envision its future place in the world. The poster child for this close connection between motricity and mentality is the sea squirt. This marine creature starts life as a motile larva, equipped with a brainlike ganglion of about 300 neurons. But after a day or two of cavorting in the shallows, the larva finds a hospitable site on the bottom and puts down roots. As a sessile organism, it has no further use for a brain, and so it eats it."

Baseball players suffer mental blocks far more often than athletes in more frenetic, less rote sports, such as football or basketball; in baseball, there's too much time to stop and think. Shortstops and third basemen rarely suffer from the problem, since their throws are nearly always somewhat rushed. For second basemen, it's the easy throw to first base that's usually the culprit, not the difficult, rushed throw from deep behind second base; for catchers, it's the even easier throw back to the pitcher. And it happens by far the most to pitchers, who, of course, have the most time to think.

Pat Jordan's memoir, *A False Spring,* chronicles his experience as a minor-league pitcher whose arm went haywire: "I could not remember how I'd once delivered a baseball with a fluid and effortless motion! And even if I could remember, I somehow knew I could never transmit that knowledge to my arms and legs, my back and shoulders. The delicate wires through which that knowledge had so often been communicated were burned out, irrevocably charred, I know now, by too much energy channeled too often along a solitary and too fragile wavelength. I lost it all that spring."

Daniel Willingham, a psychologist at the University of Virginia, makes a distinction between "implicit learning"—what the body knows—and "explicit learning"—conscious knowledge. In cases in which athletes develop mental blocks, a switch has been flipped from implicit to explicit. I played high school tennis, and I remember this happening to me once, in the district finals. I won the first set against someone who was an obviously superior player, and when I realized this fact, I suddenly couldn't get my right arm to stop moving in jagged, pixilated slow motion. I felt like a marionette operated by some unknown other. I lost the last two sets 6–1, 6–0.

Hayes says, "None of us knows—at the level of consciousness—how to walk, or breathe, or throw a baseball. If we had to take charge of these movements, issuing commands to all the hundreds of muscles in just the right sequence, who would not collapse in a quivering mass?"

"I'd never heard of 'throwing percentage' before I came to the big leagues," Texas Rangers catcher Mike Stanley said. "I got here, and that's what catchers are judged on. We had a very slow staff, but I started thinking it was me." Although he was fixated on the percentage of base stealers he threw out, Stanley—his body in full rebellion against his mind—threw soft, high-arcing tosses to second and third base whenever anyone tried to steal. "I never realized how much of the game is mental. You can see it when guys walk up to the plate, which guys are afraid. I'm sure they could see the fear in my eyes."

Rod Dishman, the director of the Exercise Psychology Lab at

the University of Georgia, says, "When thinking interferes, it physiologically, neurologically leads to inappropriate tension. That causes change in velocity and delivery. It wouldn't take much tension to throw it off. Just that split-second thought— 'God, am I going to do it again?'—can affect it."

In 1997 Rick Ankiel, whom *USA Today* named the High School Player of the Year, signed with the St. Louis Cardinals and received a $2.5 million bonus. In 1999 he was the Minor League Player of the Year. In 2000, his first full season with St. Louis, his won-loss record was 11–7, and in the last month of the season he was 4–0 with a 1.97 ERA. At age 21, he started the first game of the National League Division Series against Atlanta. In two starts and one relief appearance in the 2000 playoffs, against the Braves and the Mets, Ankiel walked 11 batters in 4 innings and threw 9 wild pitches, most of which sailed ten feet over the batters' heads. In a game against the Mets, he threw 5 of his first 20 pitches off the wire screen behind home plate. He's no longer in major-league baseball.

Ankiel says, "I was always the smallest kid. I was terribly shy. Maybe it was because my dad yelled at me so much. I was afraid to mess up. If I swung at a bad pitch in Little League, he'd make me run wind sprints when I got home. It was always, I could've done better. He always said, 'Do what I say, not what I do.'" Rick Sr. has been arrested fifteen times and convicted seven times— burglary, carrying a concealed weapon, and most recently, drug smuggling.

Ankiel says his father instructed him "never to show emotion on the mound, which I always thought was strange because I was never like that anyway."

At 14 Ankiel told his father, "I'm never going to be in the

major leagues, so I'm going to do stuff with my buddies, hang out on the beach, go surfing, go fishing" in Fort Pierce, Florida.

Ankiel's father said, "That's not gonna work. If you love the game, good things will happen."

In *The Human Motor: Energy, Fatigue, and the Origins of Modernity*, Anson Rabinbach writes: "Neurasthenia was a kind of inverted work ethic, an ethic of resistance to work in all its forms. The lack of will or energy manifested by neurasthenics is the incapacity to work productively."

When Ankiel started to have trouble throwing the ball over the plate during the 2000 playoffs, his father, Ankiel's pitching guru his entire life, had recently been sentenced to prison for six years, and his parents had just gotten divorced. With his father gone, Ankiel made sure bad things happened.

Asked how he would treat Rick Ankiel, sports psychologist Jack Llewelyn said, "You pull out vintage throws, and then you repeat those throws eight to ten times on videotape. What you're doing is bombarding the system by showing them what they're capable of doing. They've almost forgotten over time about how good they are, since they've been bombarded lately with all the negatives. If he's strong, young, and healthy, and he's thrown well in the past, then he can get past it. But anybody who thinks he can get rid of it and not think about it again probably is kidding himself. I think it's always there. I think you can do some things mentally to push it to the back. But the worst thing you can do when you start to throw better is to start to get complacent and say, 'Well, I've got that licked.'"

Shawn Havery, a sports psychologist, says about players who have suffered this problem: "I believe that they come to, kind of first off, doubt their ability. They start to overthink something that should be really reflexive. They begin to take too much time to consider all the machinations that go with that. It destroys their ability to do what they've been practicing so long."

Mets catcher Mackey Sasser had to pump the ball two or three times into his glove before lobbing the ball weakly back to the pitcher, which drove Mets pitchers to distraction and allowed opposing base runners to make delayed steals. During one game between New York and Montreal, Expos players counted Sasser's tapping of the ball into his glove, then Bronx-cheered when he finally threw the ball back to the pitcher.

When Sasser struggled in spring training in 1992, Jeff Shames wrote, "The root of Sasser's problem and mine is that we think too much about performing an ordinary chore. I stutter when I think too much about the act of speaking. All of us have difficulties in daily life. Sasser's and mine are just a little more obvious. We do what we can, even if it's not as quickly as some would like."

Former major-league manager Chuck Tanner says, "You can't be afraid to fail. If you worry about failing, you will. The biggest reason behind these throwing mysteries is players trying not to make mistakes." The same is true of stuttering. Stuttering consists of nothing but the attempt not to stutter.

Growing up in a maniacally verbal family, I placed too much emphasis on speaking; hence my stutter. A similar thing happened to many of these guys: they're almost all hypersensitive, hypertensive types; they wanted it too badly, and then their over-stressed body rebelled.

In "On Sickness," E. M. Cioran writes, "Flesh freeing itself, rebelling, no longer willing to serve, sickness in apostasy of the organs; each insists on going its own way, each, suddenly or gradually, refusing to play the game, to collaborate with the rest, hurls itself into adventure and caprice."

A lot of these guys also had overbearing stage fathers; the moment the father was dead or in prison or non compos mentis, the sons' bodies celebrated their freedom from tyranny by self-destructing.

I've never heard of a stutterer who couldn't talk fluently to himself; it's a psychosocial disorder, as are athletes' mental blocks. In both cases, the person is unable to exist in easy dialogue (conversation, catch) with another.

Mental meltdowns of this kind are not unrelated to stuttering—the blocked individual becoming self-conscious about a routine activity that everybody else takes for granted—and I think that's part of why I'm interested in the phenomenon, sympathetic to it.

The ritual of rituals, playing catch with Dad, gets problematized, and so suddenly you can't make the throw to first base, because you're thinking too much. It's as if at age 22 or 24 or 28 or 31 these athletes newly discovered the activity (worry, contemplation, self-scrutiny) that the rest of us do all the time, or at least I do all the time. For some reason they're thinking about something else—some failure or sadness or guilt or weakness—and now can't perform without thinking about performing.

Kansas City Royals catcher Fran Healy (who, like Sasser, developed a mental block about throwing the ball back to the pitcher, and who, like Wohlers, is a native of Holyoke, Massachusetts—that mindful town) said, "The easiest thing a catcher has to do is throw the ball to the pitcher. It's a thing that should be as easy as opening a door. But having to think about something that simple makes it a problem. The problem, to a degree, existed throughout my career. But I was able to hide it. I'd just flip it back real easy to the pitcher. I'd walk out after every pitch and say something like 'Stay low' or 'Keep on it' or 'Bad call.' As a catcher, you can disguise a problem like this. Pitchers can't. Their careers are over."

Dick Radatz, a Boston Red Sox relief pitcher, once threw 27 consecutive balls in a spring-training game.

Playing second base for Minnesota, Chuck Knoblauch made only 8 errors in 1996 and won the Gold Glove in 1997, maintaining a 47-game errorless streak. In 1999, playing for the Yankees, undergoing a divorce, and watching his father (his high school baseball coach and lifelong mentor) succumb to Alzheimer's, he made 26 errors, including 14 throwing errors, most of which were on routine throws to first base. On plays in which he had to hurry, Knoblauch nearly always threw the ball fine. His throwing problems inevitably occurred on routine ground balls when he had too much time to think.

"I really think, deep down inside of me, something is going on," Knoblauch said. "Something, somewhere along the line in my life, has affected me, and I don't know what it is. It's frustrating and it's puzzling. I don't ask, 'Why me?' because I'm a firm believer that everything in life happens for a reason. But I just have this feeling that whenever this thing stops, I'll know it without even picking up a baseball and throwing it. When I get to the root of this problem, I'll know I'm better without even walking on a baseball field. A lot of people have suggested that my throwing problems are going to be fixed simply by my going to left field for a while. I don't think that's going to be the case. That says this is something I can consciously correct. I know for sure it's not."

E. M. Cioran says, "Without pain, there would not be consciousness."

"If we can just get the mental part out of this thing," Yankees manager Joe Torre said about Knoblauch's throwing problem, "we'll be okay."

David Grand, the proponent of a system known as EMDR (Eye Movement Desensitization and Reprocessing), says, "The problem appears out of nowhere. It can happen a few times and go away or it may never go away. People think that when you add 'sport' to 'psychology,' the reasons change. People, even top athletes, bring to the plate all of their life experiences. The public openness of the problem, for all professional athletes, makes it much worse. EMDR reaches deep into the nervous system and lets people work on releasing traumatic memories. Patients begin to make a connection between the memory and what they are experiencing in the present. Unless you deal with the traumas, you're pulling up the weeds without the roots. Every time Ankiel makes a bad throw, it retraumatizes him. Give me three days with Ankiel, and he'll be back to where he was. Give me a week, and he'll be even better. I have no question that Knoblauch can go back to second base without the yips and return to his Gold Glove position." Knoblauch was traded to Kansas City, where he played left field for 80 games before retiring.

Another psychologist, asked how many athletes overcome these mental blocks, replied, "Very few. Almost none."

In 1957, at age 18, Von McDaniel won the first four games he pitched in the major leagues, pitched 19 consecutive scoreless innings, including a one-hitter, a two-hitter, and a perfect game for 6 innings. He finished the year at 7–5, with a 3.22 ERA. In

1958 he pitched 2 innings in which he walked 7 batters; he never pitched again in the major leagues.

Lindy McDaniel, who pitched for many years in the major leagues, said about his brother Von: "He lost his coordination and his mechanics. There was no real explanation. Some people thought it was psychological, but who knew about those things then? They sent Von down to the minors, but he couldn't get anyone out. He kept sinking further and further until he couldn't pitch anymore. It depressed him for years after he left baseball. But he couldn't talk about it."

None of these guys can talk about what's really bothering them. That's the problem. They're all repressive depressives, strong-silent types.

A student in my class, feeling self-conscious about being much older than the other students, told me that he'd been in prison. I asked him what crime he'd committed, and he said, "Shot a dude." He wrote a series of very good but very stoic stories about prison life, and when I asked him why the stories were so tight-lipped, he explained to me the jailhouse concept of "doing your own time," which means that when you're a prisoner, you're not supposed to burden the other prisoners by complaining about your incarceration or regretting what you'd done or, especially, claiming you hadn't done it. "Do your own time": it's a seductive slogan. I find that I quote it to myself occasionally, but really I don't subscribe to the sentiment. We're not, after all, in prison. Stoicism is of no use whatsoever. What I'm a big believer in is talking about everything until you're blue in the face.

Daniel Wegner, a professor of social psychology at Harvard, says, "People will develop an obsession not because there's anything interesting about it but because so much energy is paid in trying to suppress it. For some, the cure is to think about it on purpose. The thing to do is tell everybody you see. Talk about it, even laugh about it."

Detroit Tigers third baseman Darnell Coles said about the 1988 season, "The first six games of the regular season, I had three errors. Then disaster really struck. I had a three-error game in Kansas City, then a few weeks later I had three more in another game. It got to the point where I wanted to cry. I really didn't want the ball hit to me. I wanted to die. Just crawl in a hole."

In 1980, when Philadelphia won the World Series, Phillies relief pitcher Kevin Saucier—possessor of a 7–3 record and a 3.42 ERA—was named by fans the most popular Philly. He said, "I'm a hyper person, and I've always had a funny walk on me. So when I did a good job or we needed to keep loose, I wasn't afraid to show a little emotion." Traded to Detroit, he pitched even better in 1981; he had 13 saves, a 1.65 ERA, and was the best reliever in baseball at retiring the first batter he faced. In 1982, though—while his marriage was nearly unraveling—he gave up 17 walks in sixteen innings. Sent to the minor leagues, he gave up 23 walks in twenty-two innings and had an 0–4 record and an ERA of 7.36.

At the Detroit training camp the next year, Saucier said, "That strange feeling hit me again, and it seemed like things were twice as bad as before. I wasn't just missing high or low. I was missing side to side. I was throwing pitches twenty feet behind hitters. I could have hurt somebody, but then again, I never got that close. I just didn't feel right. It was like I was under a spell. It was a feeling of being lost, like trying to type with no fingers.

What do you do? You're lost. You can't help yourself. You try, you try to relax, and you can't."

Deborah Bright, a sports psychologist, says, "Too often, athletes with natural ability are not aware of what it is they do that makes them play well, and when they get off-track, they don't know what to look for. Also, few realize how much their private lives can affect their public performance." Interesting that a female psychologist points this out, since it's not a problem women are likely to have—failing to realize that their private lives can affect their public performance. So, too, women athletes are far less likely than men to be reluctant to talk about whatever might be plaguing them. It's nearly unheard of for a woman athlete to suffer from the yips. (It's also nearly unheard of for a black athlete to suffer from the yips. Absent other pressures, other oppressions, white men have a tendency to oppress themselves by overthinking.)

In James Joyce's story "The Dead," which takes place at a Christmas party, the protagonist, Gabriel Conroy, remembers a phrase from a review he wrote: "One feels that one is listening to a thought-tormented music." Later, when he gives a toast, he says, "But we are living in a sceptical and, if I may use the phrase, a thought-tormented age."

On routine plays, Monty Fariss, a minor leaguer for the Texas Rangers and a rare shortstop with this particular mind-body problem, threw timidly to first base, often allowing the batter to beat the throw, although on difficult balls into the hole at shortstop he would still make strong throws across the diamond. "Everybody wants to help solve the problem," Fariss said, "or help create one."

In the bullpen, Oakland A's pitcher Bill Mooneyham was so

afraid of throwing a wild pitch, which could roll onto the field and delay the game, that while warming up he was able to throw only changeups.

David Mamet says, "It is in our nature to elaborate, estimate, predict—to run before the event. This is the meaning of consciousness; anything else is instinct."

In 1987, a year after throwing a no-hitter, Joe Cowley of the Chicago White Sox gave up 21 hits, 17 walks, and 20 earned runs in less than 12 innings. He never regained his form.

In 1971 Steve Blass won 15 games for the Pittsburgh Pirates, with a 2.85 ERA, and won the third, then the deciding seventh game of the World Series. In 1972 he won 19 games, lost 8, pitched 11 complete games, had an ERA of 2.48, sixth best in the National League, and was an all-star. Throughout his career he had allowed fewer than 3 walks per 9 innings.

During spring training in 1973, he walked 25 men in 14 innings, throwing one pitch that was so wild it nearly landed in the third-base dugout. In the 1973 season, Blass was 3–9 with a 9.85 ERA, walking 84 batters in fewer than 89 innings. He tried pitching from the outfield. He tried pitching while kneeling on the mound. He tried pitching with his left foot tucked up behind his right knee. He tried Transcendental Meditation. He studied slow-motion films of his delivery. Warming up or throwing on the sidelines, while working alone with a catcher, he pitched well, but the moment a batter stood in against him, he struggled, especially with his fastball. Blass was permanently out of baseball after that year.

Blass recently said, "I still can't pitch, not even at my own baseball camp."

There were many theories about Blass: he was too nice, he

lost his will to win, his mechanics were off, his eyesight deteriorated, he was afraid of being hit by a line drive, he was afraid of injuring a batter with a fastball, the death of his superstar teammate Roberto Clemente incapacitated him, a slump led to a loss of self-confidence, which led to a worse slump, which led to less self-confidence. . . .

Dave Giusti, Blass's close friend and a fellow pitcher, said about Blass, "He is remarkably open to all kinds of people, but I think he has closed his mind to his inner self. There are central areas you can't infringe on with him. There is no doubt that during the past two years he didn't react to a bad performance the way he used to, and you have to wonder why he couldn't apply his competitiveness to his problem. Last year I went through something like Steve's crisis. The first half of the season, I was atrocious, and I lost all my confidence, especially in my fastball. I began worrying about making big money and not performing. I worried about not contributing to the team. I worried about being traded. I thought it might be the end for me. I didn't know how to solve my problem, but I knew I had to solve it. In the end, it was talking to people that did it. I talked to everybody. Then, at some point, I turned the corner. But it was talking that did it, and my point is that Steve can't talk to people that way. Or won't."

In *Intoxicated by My Illness,* Anatole Broyard writes: "The patient has to start by treating his illness not as a disaster, an occasion for depression or panic, but as a narrative, a story. Stories are antibodies against illness and pain. When various doctors shoved scopes up my urethral canal, I found that it helped a lot when they gave me a narrative of what they were doing. Their talking translated or humanized the procedure. It prepared, strengthened, and somehow consoled me. Anything is better than an awful silent suffering."

Los Angeles Dodgers second baseman Steve Sax—after overcoming such a severe case of the yips (30 errors by mid-August in 1983) that it became known for a while as Steve Sax Disease—said, "It's a matter of eliminating all possibility of error as far as mechanics go. Get that down pat, make good throws, and get your confidence back."

The Dodgers tied a sock over Sax's eyes and made him throw balls to first base blindfolded.

The Tigers had Coles throw sidearm.

The Mets had Sasser practice throwing from his knees.

When Philadelphia Phillies pitcher Bruce Ruffin lost his control in 1988, a fan suggested that he take the can of chewing tobacco out of his back pocket.

Everybody tells a player with a mental block not to think about it.

Sax said, "It's like a big elephant in front of you. You can't ignore it."

Sasser said, "I've been working with people on visualization. But either the throw's going to come or it's not. What can you do? Just pray."

Mike Stanley said, "All I could visualize was making an errant throw. I couldn't even visualize making a good one."

In the Land of Pain is Alphonse Daudet's diary of the disintegration of his body (and fellow sufferers' bodies) from neurosyphilis. "No general theory about pain," he writes. "Each patient discovers his own, and the nature of pain varies, like a singer's voice, according to the acoustics of the hall."

Nobody's perfect.

Everybody's human.

A magazine editor putting together a how-to issue asked if there was any activity about which I wanted to write a how-to article. "How about a how-not-to?" I replied. There are so many things I can't do—just for starters: blow a bubble, dive, whistle, snap my fingers.

Woody Allen says, "Basically, everybody is a loser, but it's only now that people are beginning to admit it."

Success has many fathers; failure is an orphan.

In the fairy tale, sport is supposed to be some sort of transcendence, a liftoff from life's travails.

The mind is a powerful thing.

The director John Cassavetes supported himself by acting in commercial movies. He said that he could take almost any line and make it interesting as long as he was allowed to put pauses in. In other words, to insert thinking.

Everybody's an expert.

Nobody knows anything.

"We work in the dark," Henry James wrote. "We do what we can. We give what we have. Our doubt is our passion and our passion is our task. The rest is the madness of art."

BEING RANDOM IS THE
KEY TO LIFE

One day, we had a discussion in class. They asked me, where did they go? The trees, the salamander, the tropical fish, Edgar, the poppas and mommas, Matthew and Tony, where did they go? And I said, I don't know, I don't know. And they said, who knows? and I said, nobody knows. And they said, is death that which gives meaning to life? And I said, no, life is that which gives meaning to life. Then they said, but isn't death, considered as a fundamental datum, the means by which the taken-for-granted mundanity of the everyday may be transcended in the direction of—

I said, yes, maybe.

They said, we don't like it.

—DONALD BARTHELME, "THE SCHOOL"

EVERYBODY'S AN EXPERT? NOBODY KNOWS ANYTHING? FAIL-ure is the only subject? Exhibit 247:

Asked to cite the best advice she's ever heard, University of Washington women's basketball player Loree Payne said, "Live in the present; you can't change the past, and the future has enough worries of its own"—which bears absolutely no relationship to how she actually lives her life. She seems to have been born with an ongoing nostalgia for parting, a sense that "life is precious, and your time is short." A graduating senior, she said, early in the 2002–2003 season, "I know that the games are getting limited, as far as how many I have left. I know the seniors are all starting to feel that way, so we're going to play every game like it's our last, because pretty soon it's going to be. There's definitely a sense of urgency to this season. You think about it every time you step on the floor, how this year is winding down." She frequently mentions being aware of the last time she'll take certain road trips, play in certain arenas, perform particular routines, do particular drills. She's a hypersensitive seismograph attuned to the earthquake of loss.

Payne says, "I kind of like everything-works-out movies"— *Top Gun, Notting Hill, You've Got Mail.* Her head coach, June Daugherty, calls her a "perfectionist." She graduated number one in her class in high school and was a member of the National Honor Society. She can't abide the emptiness of chaos, which she fills with faith. Her pregame ritual is to "relax and pray, giving the game to God." She wears a wristband that says "Sisters in Christ." When she was asked who the most influential person in her life is, she replied, "Jesus." When she was asked to name three people whom she would like to invite to dinner, she named Jesus, Job, and Paul. All of her favorite singers and bands are "Christian contemporary": Jennifer Knapp, Third Day, Jars of Clay, Souljahz, Priesthood. The quotation at the end of her e-mails is: "You will seek Me and find Me when you seek Me with all your heart. (Jeremiah 29:13)." Another favorite quotation is: "Do not trust in your own understanding; in all your ways acknowledge Him and He will direct your path."

Asked, at the beginning of the season, who her funniest teammate is, Payne named her best friend, "Kayla Burt, because she's the most random person I know." Another player, Kirsten Brockman, said, "My funniest teammate is Kayla. She brings out the five-year-old in me and everyone." Kristen O'Neill answered, "Everyone can make me laugh, but Kayla is definitely the biggest spaz." Nicole Castro said, "My funniest teammate is Kayla, for sure. She just comes out with the strangest things." Asked for the best advice she'd ever heard, Burt said, "Being random is the key to life."

HERE'S HOW KEY to life being random is:

On New Year's Eve 2002, Burt and several of her teammates had a party at her house. Since they had an 8:30 a.m. practice the next day—punishment for a lackadaisical practice on December 31—there wasn't a lot of carousing: they ordered pizza, ate junk food, looked at high school yearbooks, told stories, and watched the substandard kidnap thriller they'd rented, *Trapped* ("You think you live in a world where no little girls are killed; I'm the one that decides if your little girl lives or dies").

Throughout the evening, Burt had complained that she didn't feel right, but, according to Payne, "she's not a complainer, and it was just something she mentioned. I went up to Kayla's room to look at the eleven o'clock news. Everyone else was downstairs. Then she came up. I was lying on her bed, and she was sitting next to me. She said, 'Loree, I feel light-headed,' and she kind of fell back, off the bed. I said, 'Kayla, get up.' Kayla is a clown and

I told her to get up. I thought she was having a seizure. I yelled to everyone to get upstairs, and Giuliana [Mendiola, the star of the team and Pac-10 Player of the Year] called 911."

Mendiola says, "When we went up there, I got around to the other side. There wasn't very much space; there were boxes and it was a really cramped space, so we just moved the boxes and all the stuff. She wasn't unconscious at that point. She was gurgling and her eyes were kind of rolling back. So we were like, 'Kayla!' She wasn't saying hello or anything. She wasn't responding."

Burt's heart had stopped.

Mendiola says, "We looked at her, and it was obvious she wasn't joking around. We slapped her face to wake her up. We rolled her over: she was purple and she needed oxygen." Mendiola pumped Burt's chest; her sister, Gioconda, gave her mouth-to-mouth. "We didn't really know what we were doing. We were just doing what we remembered from TV shows." *Rescue 911* was Kayla's favorite show.

Gioconda says, "I was just blowing into her mouth. Her chest was going up and down and she gasped, so I guessed it was working."

Erica Schelly repeated CPR instructions from the Medic One operator on the phone: "Fifteen compressions to the chest, then two breaths."

"I had no idea what to do," Schelly says. "I was freaking out. The only thing that kept me sane was having this to do. I was pretty scared."

Burt didn't have a pulse. She wheezed; her body shook.

Paramedics—including Michelle Perkins, a former Washington basketball player who is now an EMT—arrived within five minutes of the 911 call.

Schelly said, "Loree and I went outside and we looked at each other and we were just like, 'Oh my gosh, what are we going to do?' And we were just like, 'What can we do? Let's just go pray, you know?' So we went outside and sat down together and prayed a little bit and went back in."

THE AMBULANCE rushed Burt to the hospital. All of the players spent the rest of that night and most of New Year's Day in the hospital. They were scheduled to travel to Los Angeles for a game against UCLA the next day, but with Burt unconscious, they didn't know whether to cancel the game.

Daugherty says, "They weren't going to leave Seattle until they had a chance to talk to Kayla and make sure she was okay, and she knew they were going to go down there and compete for her."

Late in the afternoon on New Year's Day, Burt began exhibiting consciousness.

Burt told a reporter, "I had something wrong with my heart, but I don't really remember anything. I guess I was talking and responding, but I don't remember a thing. I'm doing a lot better, though."

Her father said, "Kayla is doing well right now. We're waiting on some test results, and that's about it. It's very difficult to see your daughter hooked up to machines and tubes and a ventilator."

Teammate Kristen O'Neill, who'd been her rival throughout high school, says she told her that "she'd had a baby, named Angelica. She knew she didn't have a baby, but it was funny, like, 'You have Angelica Baby in your room.'"

Payne says, "Our team gave her a card. She got it and she read it. She'd read one side and laugh at certain people's jokes, then she'd read the back, then she'd go back and read the front again. For, seriously, like, ten minutes, she kept reading it, and we were, like, 'Okay, enough.'

"She asked if we won the game. We told her we hadn't played yet. She said, 'Why not, because of me?' We said, 'No, the game isn't until tomorrow.' She told us to play and win."

Before their game against UCLA on Friday (postponed one day), Burt told Payne to tell their teammates: "I love you guys. Think about me, but don't think about me too much. Just play like you know how."

Wearing white armbands with "#20" or "Kayla Burt" or "Get well, Kayla," they shot 24 percent from the field and lost 74–46—their worst loss in two years.

Payne says, "We could have told her that we won, because she doesn't remember."

That Sunday night, though, they rallied from an 11-point deficit to beat USC in overtime.

Burt says, "I sat in my hospital room and listened on the radio. I'd never heard an actual radio broadcast before of our games, because I've always been playing. They could easily have crumpled and played horrible under the circumstances, but they came out and played their hearts out for me. For them to pull that out and to know that they did that for me, that was awesome."

In her postgame press conference, Daugherty said, "Every kid that stepped on the court just left it all out there. Most of the game, we were on the floor more than we were standing up, trying to save loose balls, helping our teammates out. In the second half, we had no energy. Every time-out, we were trying to rotate kids and remind them that they're playing for Kayla and that they have to get their energy on defense and get stops. To see them have the courage to compete and work that hard for Kayla—it's my proudest moment ever as a coach because they played a game for the right reasons. They played it for their teammate. The amount of effort and love that they put out there was amazing. They willed the win for Kayla."

Payne, who scored 17 points, said, "It was the biggest win of my career, and we went to the Elite Eight [in 2001]. It wasn't because of basketball. It was how this team came together, fought through, and was ultimately bonded by this experience. This has truly changed everybody. We have huge goals as a team, but this makes you realize the important things in life. Everybody needs a perspective check here and there. We got a big one." Payne always seems to say the correct thing and do what she's supposed to do, as if she were perpetually running for election.

SIX DAYS AFTER Burt's heart stopped, doctors diagnosed her with Long QT syndrome and implanted an automatic defibrillator in her chest—a device that monitors the heartbeat and applies a shock if irregularities are detected. The implant monitors her heart rhythm and emits an electrical shock to restore a normal rhythm should another abnormality occur.

At a press conference the next day, her cardiologist, Peter Kudenchuk, said, "Long QT is a genetic abnormality of the heart that can predispose people to sudden and unexplained and dangerous heart rhythms." *She's the most random person I've ever met.* "Kayla is a real trooper and gave the high-five both going in to surgery and when she came out. I told her not to do the high-five on the right side, because that's where we put the defibrillator." The defibrillator, inserted on her right side because she's left-handed, will allow her to live a normal life, but she still has a 20 percent chance of a repeat episode in the next year, and her basketball career is over.

Burt said, "I am about as lucky as anyone has ever been lucky. My heart was stopped; I was dead. I've gone through so much in just the past week. I feel so blessed by everyone, and I am here and I am happy. I have amazing teammates. I can't say it enough, how much I—they're my sisters for life."

Daugherty said, "Hopefully, we will have Kayla back in school this quarter. It sounds like that is something the doctors think she can do. The sooner we can get her back in the arena and with the team, the better. We haven't had the opportunity to sit down and talk about it, but she will certainly remain on scholarship and remain on this team and be a huge part of this basketball family. At some point, hopefully, I can recruit her to be some kind of student assistant coach. We will get to that when we get her a little bit stronger and out of the hospital."

Assistant coach Mike Daugherty, June's husband, said about Burt, "She was such a perfect basketball player. She could have been the best one we ever had." A sophomore averaging 10 points and 4 rebounds a game, she was leading the Pac-10 in 3-point field-goal percentage and assist-to-turnover ratio.

Teri Burt, Kayla's mother, said about her five teammates, "They were so courageous. They did what they needed to do and basically saved my daughter's life. For that, I will be forever grateful."

Payne said, "Under a pressure situation, what do you do? Being a student-athlete, you learn the concept of team and the concept of composure, and they definitely came into play. We can play the 'What if' game. I've done that. Believe me. I've done it a lot and made myself scared. 'What if I had gone downstairs?' 'What if I wasn't there?' But I *was* there. And there was a reason I was there." The Head Coach has a plan for all of us.

TEN DAYS AFTER her cardiac arrest, Burt returned to the arena. Wearing a red coat, a white turtleneck, black slacks, and high heels, she looked radiant as she stood along the baseline before the game, high-fiving everyone in sight as Washington and Arizona State warmed up. A camera crew from *Inside Edition* followed her everywhere she went.

At the beginning of the game, she walked with three teammates to center court to serve as an honorary captain. When the starting lineups were announced, she was introduced as a special "sixth starter." She received a prolonged, passionate, standing ovation from the crowd of 4,000—the largest crowd of the year. "Just to walk out there was really special. To hear that roar when I came out, it hits you real close, and it's awesome."

Signs in the crowd, held mainly by teenage girls wearing their basketball uniforms, said "Burt," "20," "Eastlake Girls Basketball Will Always Remember Kayla Burt," "Heroines of the Hardwood," "We Love Kayla."

"I want to do everything I can to be normal," she said.

Her 17-year-old brother said, "There's nothing normal about you."

Washington won, pushing its overall record to 11–2, 3–1 during the Pac-10 season. Giuliana Mendiola, celebrating her twenty-first birthday, scored 22 points, had 10 rebounds and 5 assists, and later said, "I was just out there trying to have fun and win the game for Kayla."

Whenever her teammates made a nice play—Payne threw a showy, behind-the-back pass on a 2-on-1 break, which sent the crowd into a frenzy—Burt stood and pumped her left fist; her right arm was still sore from the surgery. Burt said, "It seemed like every little thing was so exciting to me. Taking a charge, creating a turnover, hitting a good shot—just the little things were so awesome to me. I can't even say enough about how hard the girls played, how tough they were, and just how inspiring it was for me to be on the bench and be a part of it. I'm just so pumped to be out there. I keep a smile on my face because I'm so happy. Life is so awesome. I'm here."

After the game, Burt, surrounded by mics and cameras, addressed the crowd, and wished Giuliana a happy birthday. The Mendiola sisters presented her with a drawing of themselves and Burt, who said afterward, "We're as close as we can ever be. They gave me CPR. I mean, how close can you get? We'll stay that way forever." They walked off the floor arm in arm.

These young women—Burt and all of her teammates—are used to being told what to do and where to go by coaches, university officials, sponsors, professors, parents, and now they're being instructed by *Inside Edition,* Connie Chung, Lifetime, *Good Housekeeping,* and ESPN. They're the media darlings of the moment, the belles of the b-ball, objects of ceaseless attention by a (nearly exclusively) male sportswriting corps, and they never turn down a media request. They can't get enough of it; they're addicted to it; they know the red light will turn off soon enough.

• • •

A COUPLE OF WEEKS later, Daugherty called a meeting, ostensibly to announce to the team that it was nationally ranked in the top 25 but actually to surprise Burt with a visit by (then) Seattle Sonics player Desmond Mason, whom Burt, in the Washington media guide, had identified as the player whose autograph she'd most like to have. He brought her a signed jersey and tickets to the Sonics game that night. At first Burt didn't recognize him. "I'm so embarrassed," she said. "I had no idea. He came on the court, and when I figured it all out, I was like, 'Oh, gosh. This is so cool.'"

Mason said, "I heard about the situation and what happened. I'm happy to see that she's okay, still in great spirits, with great friends around her. I'm just here to tell her I appreciate her, and I'm glad she's okay."

Then Burt challenged Mason to a game of H-O-R-S-E. Her first shot was from beyond the 3-point line. Swish. Mason's attempt clanged off the rim. He took off his baseball cap and teased her—"Is this a women's ball?"—but she kept shooting threes and couldn't miss and he kept missing and she won going away.

On and especially off the court, other players look to Payne to lead. She's the team captain and was the team spokeswoman at various press conferences following Burt's hospitalization. At these press conferences, Payne seemed to make a particular point of holding her head high, maintaining a tight smile. "I like being in situations where people look to me to direct," she says. "I'm ready for that. It's a natural role for me." When her playing career is over, she plans to coach; she's a psychology major because she thinks it will provide a good foundation for coaching. (After graduating with a 3.6 GPA, she went straight to an assistant coaching position at Northwest Nazarene University, in Nampa, Idaho, where she's studying for her master's in school counseling.)

On New Year's Eve, Payne called downstairs to her teammates, then waited outside to guide the ambulance toward the house, but it was Giuliana Mendiola who called 911, and freshman Erica Schelly who relayed instructions from the emergency operator; it was the Mendiola sisters who performed CPR on Payne's best friend. Payne's game is the same. The sixth best scorer in UW history, she's an excellent shooter, especially from long range, but that's all she does. She's an average passer, can't penetrate to the basket, doesn't rebound, doesn't defend. "I know false hustle when I see it," Boston Celtics coach Red Auerbach once said. False hustle is her M.O. on defense. She doesn't work hard for or hold her position on either end of the floor. As a senior, she possesses exactly the same strengths and weaknesses she possessed as an incoming freshman. She's not very flexible or quick, has sloppy footwork, often cherry-picks to try to get an easy basket off the break, is monomaniacally focused on her own shooting (doesn't follow her own shot, usually claps to herself whenever she scores, grimaces when she misses). She rarely fights for a loose ball, stays away from the scrum, isn't scrappy. For all of her reported selflessness off the court (she frequently visits Children's Hospital and Ronald McDonald House; Daugherty says, "She has a great spirit about her—she genuinely cares about people—I can't even begin to talk about how much community service she does"), on the court she seems to be quite self-centered. This doesn't make her a hypocrite or a bad person. It just makes her a person: full of the contradictions, confusions, internal dramas, and mysteries that anyone else has and that she has trouble accepting about herself.

"As I was growing up, even with success in basketball and

school and a great family, there was still something missing," Payne says, "but I couldn't put my finger on it. Once God opened my eyes to the fact that He was the thing missing in my life, I became complete. There is a God-place in all of us; it's the only thing that could ever possibly give anyone true happiness. Now I find that basketball is not my entire life; it's only something that is a part of my life, and for that I am so thankful. I just have a different perspective now, an eternal one that really allows me to prioritize things. Not saying, by any means, that I have it all together. That is the awesome thing about God: He gives us grace because we *don't* have it all together. Within this process, the more knowledge I gain, the more I realize how little I know. It is awesome, though!"

In e-mails, Payne's partial to the single, double, and even triple exclamation point. It's important to her to be—and to be perceived to be—positive, upbeat, Christ-fueled. To me it's an interesting, open, and utterly unanswerable question: to what degree does she believe the bland reassurances she articulates for public consumption? Or, more precisely: what is the relation between these reassurances and what she actually feels in her heart of hearts? I would think this would be a difficult question even for her to answer. The bun she tucks her hair into on game days is hard as a fist.

Shooters win games and obtain the podium, while somebody else does the dirty work. One thing Christ was teaching his disciples was to do the dirty work, and they were having a hard time with it. Who wouldn't, after a few miracles?

THE HUSKIES' 2002–03 record was 22–8; they placed second in the Pac-10, then were eliminated in the first round of the NCAA

tournament. Payne was chosen All-Pac-10 for the second straight
year. She averaged 16 points and shot 51 percent from the field
before New Year's Eve, 13 points and 40 percent after. She says, "I
kind of went through a drought where it was hard to focus in class
and on the court. I didn't feel like my natural self as a player or
anything. I was trying a little too hard to get over it, because this
type of thing takes time, facing the conflicting things within me.
Most people don't experience something like this in their entire
life, so it's not like, 'Oh, well, she's okay, so everything's okay.' I
don't know how many people heard it, but Michelle [Perkins, the
EMT and former Washington player] went, 'We lost her, but we
brought her back.' Kayla died for a second. She was no longer
with us. That was reality, right there. I was just, like, 'Whoa, hold
on.' It wasn't like, 'Oh, she was never going to . . .' She was very
going to." Loree Payne is half in love with easeful death.

ONE NIGHT IN late February, a couple of days before their final
game of the regular season, Burt and Payne sit in the living room
of Burt's rental house, which she shares with three teammates.

Burt says about Payne, "She needs to know what's going on.
She needs to know the plan, and I'm just like, 'Whatever. Let me
know.' There will be times when she's freaking out and I'm like,
'Loree, relax.' I'll just say things out of the blue. That's just kind
of my personality. I keep her on her toes. When we drive in her
car and she's parking, she has to get it perfectly straight. And I'm
like: 'It's fine!' She'll pack for trips five days in advance, and I'll
pack ten minutes before we go."

Payne says, "Just thinking about how close she came to being
removed from our lives—I think that's the most difficult thing.

You hear that ninety-five percent of people who go through this don't live. And if it would have been two minutes longer, she would have had brain damage and not been normal again. I would have been losing my best friend. It's the hardest when you're alone, reflecting on it, and you start to let the negative thoughts come in. I know I'm still dealing with it every single day, and it's hard. It takes time. If you drop her off at her house and no one's here, it's a fear that you never should have, but you do. Or you call on the cell phone and she doesn't answer and you're like, 'Aargh, why didn't she answer?' Those are feelings that normal people don't have. Things like this happen to other people. They don't happen to you."

Burt says, "It seems like every single thing that took place that night was perfect. I could have gone upstairs by myself and Loree wouldn't have been there. None of the other girls could have been here. Even where I live: the fire station is right down the road, and I think that that was huge—how it only took them about four minutes to get to my house. It's all those little things that you don't really think about are so important and were so important in everything that happened that night."

Payne says, "I don't believe in coincidences. Things like that don't just happen, you know. It was supposed to happen that way, and there was no other way it possibly could have happened. You just have to trust in that, and that is what faith is all about, because you can't hear about everything that happened, and think: 'Oh, good thing it happened that way.' Or, 'That was a good chance.' That is not possible.

"At our church, the pastor gave an altar call, where he asks what it means to be a Christian. Kayla gave her testimony, and eighteen people came to know the Word. It was awesome how

God used Kayla to do that. Anyone who went through this situation and to be as joyous as she's been since the day she left the hospital—there's something special. If someone didn't believe in God before this, I don't see how anyone couldn't now. She's a walking witness. She's God's miracle."

Burt says, "I can honestly say I love every single person on this team and all the coaches and all the members of my family. It's so important to let the people that you love know, because those could be your last words, and that's why I don't feel ashamed or embarrassed to tell people that I love them, and if anything were to happen to any of these people, I'd want them to know how I feel about them. You gotta say things that are on your mind, because you never know.

"Yeah, it was a very serious thing that happened in my life, but the fact that it's over with and I'm basically back to normal physically, I can joke around about it and talk about it. It's not a big deal for me at all. I never even really thought about death. I mean, yeah, I heard that I actually did die and that I was brought back, but I don't think about that anymore. I've never really thought about it, just because I am alive and so it's like, why even think about that, you know?"

Tugging down the right side of her sweatshirt a little and displaying her defibrillator, which she explains is only 1" × 1", she says, "I don't even really notice it. It just hangs out a little. It's good. It's pretty cool."

Payne, trying to imitate Burt's jokey style, measures the defibrillator with her fingers and keeps insisting that it's at least 2" × 2" (in fact, it's 1" × 1½"). Payne's joking isn't funny, though: she doesn't comprehend that Burt's a little defensive about the size of this silver device sticking out of her chest.

In a similar way, when Burt is asked what she's going to do now that her basketball career is over and she hesitates for a moment, Payne says, "Academics."

Burt talks about how pitifully unprepared Connie Chung was when she interviewed her, and how Daugherty has a tendency to get things wrong—which magazine is interviewing whom, where they're meeting, etc.—and at first when Payne says, "Shut up," she seems to be teasing, but when Burt continues to undermine these authority figures, Payne—big sister, team captain, traffic advisory—repeats, with emphasis, "No. Really. Shut up."

In the Washington media guide, asked who would play themselves in a movie, Burt said Cameron Diaz; Payne said Meg Ryan.

Funny, niceness; lightness, loss; life-lunging, death-trapped.

In *Trapped*, explaining his kidnapping plan to his six-year-old victim, Kevin Bacon says, "This is a machine that runs on fear."

Though occasionally, at Payne's behest, Burt gestures in the direction of religion, she seems to know she's only bones and blood; Payne thinks Burt's body is a vessel of God.

Burt thinks people saved her; Payne is certain of divine intervention.

Payne believes, anxiously, in order; Burt knows that being random is the key to life.

42 TATTOOS: AN EPILOGUE

A TATTOO IS INK STORED IN SCAR TISSUE.

ARCHEOLOGISTS BELIEVE, based on marks they've seen on mummies, that human beings had tattoos between 4000 and 2000 B.C. in Egypt. Around 2000 B.C., tattooing spread to southern Asia to Japan and from there to Burma and Scythia.

IN 1998, 35 percent of NBA players had tattoos. Now, well over 50 percent have tattoos. According to the *Christian Science Monitor*, that arbiter of the down and dirty, the number of Americans with tattoos is "as high as 15 percent."

ASKED BY *PLAYBOY* what he'd like people to know, Allen Iverson said, "Tell them not to believe what they read or hear. Tell them to read my body. I wear my story every day, man." At the very end of the interview, Iverson said, "The minister at [his close friend] Rah's funeral said to look at your life as a book and stop wasting pages complaining, worrying, and gossiping. That's some deep shit right there."

IN BODY-CONTACT sports, such as basketball or football, there's a much higher percentage of tattooed players than in "cerebral" sports, such as baseball, golf, or tennis.

A COUPLE YEARS AGO, while watching a basketball game on TV, Dakkan Abbe, a marketing executive with the advertising firm Fifty Rubies, came up with the idea of NBA players selling space on their bodies to plug products with temporary tattoos. Abbe wanted someone with "bad boy" appeal, so he approached Rasheed Wallace, who the previous year had set an NBA record for the most technical fouls in a season, about a candy-bar tattoo. Wallace's agent, Bill Strickland, said there's "nothing in any basic agreement [between the players' association and the league] that forbids advertising on the human body." An NBA spokesman said, "We don't allow commercial advertising on our uniforms, our coaches, or our playing floors, so there's no reason to think we'll allow it on our players." Abbe said, "The NBA is defining tattoos as part of the players' uniforms, but a player's skin is not part of his uniform. I find it offensive that the league would not allow something on someone's skin. Whenever the topic of tatoos comes up, the league says things like, 'We prefer if players didn't have tattoos.' The NBA scared people off. The very nature of tattoos is disturbing to the NBA. The league is a little bit out of touch with the players and fans. Tattoos are a very explicit example of that. They just don't understand what tattoos are about." Strickland said, "Being a lawyer, I thought it presented some free-speech issues," but he finally decided not to press the case. Stephon Marbury of the New York Knicks, asked if he'd wear a tattoo advertisement, said, "Depends on how much money they'd pay. If they're paying the right money: yeah." Selling, say, his left shoulder to a shoe company, would Stephon Marbury be losing control over his body or exerting control over capitalism?

IN THE *TATTOO* magazine supplement to the New Orleans tattoo convention, an inordinately buxom but somehow slightly demure-looking blond babe is on the cover, wearing a sailor hat, fishnet stockings, a short red skirt, white gloves, a bra top, and a couple of tattoos. Behind her, in black shadow, is a dark-haired woman dressed in a leopard costume. The function of the blond babe's tattoos is to portray her in the process of being transfigured from sailor girl to jungle cat and back again (and to portray as well the eros of this tension between civilization and savagery).

"AS FOR THE PRIMITIVE, I hark back to it because we are still very primitive. How many thousands of years of culture, think you, have rubbed and polished at our raw edges? One probably; at the best, no more than two. And that takes us back to screaming savagery, when, gross of body and deed, we drank blood from the skulls of our enemies and hailed as highest paradise the orgies and carnage of Valhalla."

—Jack London

ACCORDING TO A third-century B.C. account of the Scythians' defeat of the Thracians, the Scythians tattooed symbols of defeat upon the Thracians, but as a way of turning "the stamp of violence and shame into beautiful ornaments," the Thracian women covered the rest of their bodies with tattoos.

ON MY THIRTIETH birthday, under my girlfriend's influence, I got my left ear pierced and bought a diamond earring. I wore various earrings over the next ten years, but wearing an earring never really worked for me, and on my fortieth birthday, under the influence of my daughter, who thought it made me look like a pirate, I took out the ring I was then wearing—a gold hoop— and I haven't worn an earring since. Earrings forced me to confront the nature of my style, or lack of style. I'm certainly not macho enough to wear an earring as if I were a tough guy, but neither am I effeminate enough to wear an earring in my right ear as if I were maybe gay-in-training. Instead, I'm just me, muddling through in the middle, and the earring forced me, over time, to see this, acknowledge it, and respond to it.

MARCUS CAMBY'S first name is tattooed on his arm; Kirby Puckett also has his first name tattooed on his arm. Scottie Pippen has small tattoos on his biceps and legs. Michael Jordan has a horseshoe-shaped fraternity tattoo. Dennis Rodman's tattoos include a Harley, a shark, a cross (the loop of which encircles his pierced navel), and a photo of his daughter. Mike Tyson has a tattoo of Che Guevara on his abdomen, a tattoo of Mao on his right hand, and one of Arthur Ashe on his left shoulder. Shaquille O'Neal has a Superman tattoo on his left shoulder. Detroit Pistons center Ben Wallace has a tattoo of the Big Ben clock tower on his right biceps, with basketballs for clock faces; he also has two tattoos of Taz, the Tasmanian devil from *Bugs Bunny*.

"HUMAN BARCODES are hip," declared that arbiter of hip, the *Wall Street Journal*. "Heavy-metal band Slipknot has a barcode logo, with the stripes emblazoned across their prison-jumpsuit outfits. Barcode tattoos are also big, says New York tattoo tycoon Carlo Fodera."

WHO OWNS THESE WORDS?

IN GALATIANS 6:17, St. Paul says, "From this time onward let no one trouble me; for, as for me, I bear, branded on my body, the scars of Jesus as my Master."

"SINCE A TATTOO to certain levels of society is the mark of a thug, it becomes also the sign of inarticulate revolt, often producing its only possible result: violence."

—Samuel Steward

IN ORDER TO demonstrate their corporate loyalty, many Nike employees wear on their leg a tattoo of a swoosh.

THE GREEK philosopher Bion of Borysthenes (c. 300 B.C.) described the brutally tattooed face of his father, a former slave, as "a narrative of his master's harshness."

JASON RICHARDSON, of the Golden State Warriors, said, "If you're a good basketball player, you've got to have some tattoos to go with the package. Basketball players have tattoos; that's the way it is. It's a way of showing who I am."

ASKED WHAT HIS tattoos mean, Iverson replied, "I got 'Cru Thik' in four places—that's my crew, that's what we call ourselves, me and the guys I grew up with, the guys I'm loyal to. I got my kids' names, Tiaura and Deuce [Allen II], 'cause they're everything to me. I got my wife's name, Tawanna, on my stomach. A set of praying hands between my grandma's initials—she died when I was real young—and my mom's initials, Ethel Ann Iverson. I put shit on my body that means something to me. Here, on my left shoulder, I got a cross of daggers knitted together that says 'only the strong survive,' because that's the one true thing I've learned in this life. On the other arm, I got a soldier's head. I feel like my life has been a war and I'm a soldier in it. Here, on my left forearm, it says 'NBN'—for 'Newport Bad News.' That's what we call our hometown of Newport News, Virginia, because a lot of bad shit happens there. On the other arm, I got the Chinese symbol for respect, because I feel that where I come from deserves respect—being from there, surviving from there, and staying true to everybody back there. I got one that says 'fear no one,' a screaming skull with a red line through it—'cause you'll never catch me looking scared."

IVERSON'S PHILADELPHIA 76er teammate Aaron McKie said, "A lot of guys get tattoos because they think they look nice and sexy wearing them. But I don't need them. One reason is because of my old college coach, John Cheney. He didn't allow players to wear tattoos or earrings or stuff like that. The other reason is because I guess I'm old-fashioned. I don't see any good reason to pierce or paint my body. I'm comfortable with my natural look."

"THE PUBLICATION of 'International Archives of Body Techniques' would be of truly international benefit, providing an inventory of all the possibilities of the human body and of the methods of apprenticeship and training employed to build up each technique, for there is not one human group in the world which could not make an original contribution to such an enterprise. It would also be a project eminently well fitted to counteracting racial prejudices, since it would contradict the racialist conceptions which try to make out that man is a product of his body, by demonstrating that it is the other way around: man has, at all times and in all places, been able to turn his body into a product of his techniques and his representations."
—Claude Lévi-Strauss

WHAT LÉVI-STRAUSS means, I think, is this: before we started, she said she needed to tell me something. She had herpes. Madly in love with her witchy bitchiness, I found occasional enforced celibacy insanely erotic, the way a chastity belt glamorizes what it locks out. We wound up living together, and as we fell out of love with each other, her herpes became a debate point between us. She suggested that we just get married and then if I got it, I got it, and who would care? I suggested she at least explore some of the possibilities of which modern medicine avails us. For a multitude of reasons, the two of us didn't belong together, but what interests me now is what, for a lack of a better term, a free-floating signifier the virus was. When I was in love with her, it eroticized her. When I wasn't, it repelled me. The body has no meanings. We bring meanings to it.

RETIRED DETROIT LIONS fullback Brock Olivo, who has only one tattoo—an Italian flag, on his back, to honor his ancestry—said, "That's my last tattoo. No more. I don't want to scare my kids or affect things in the business world by having all kinds of crazy stuff on me."

ACCORDING TO *Rolling Stone*, Paul Booth is "the tattoo artist of choice for rock stars who love death, perversion, and torture." His "black-and-gray tattoos of blasphemous violence echo the same nihilist madness of the metalheads he inks"—musicians from Slipknot, Mudvayne, Slayer, Pantera, and Soulfly. His East Village shop features cobwebs, rusty meat hooks, a moose head, a mummified cat, medieval torture devices, a gynecologist's black leather chair with silver stirrups, a human skull given to him by a Swedish gravedigger, a note from a customer written in blood. Booth's arms are covered in tattoos, his face is studded with silver loops, and he's enormously fat. Some of his most popular tattoos are "weeping demons, decapitated Christ figures, transvestite nuns severing their own genitals, cascading waves of melting skulls, muscled werewolves raping bare-chested women." He has a two-year waiting list. His clients—including the "hardcore-metal elite"—come to him "because they share his frustration and rage, his feelings of anger and alienation. He understands those emotions and brings them to the surface with his needle. His gift lies in transforming the dark side of his clients—their hurt, their torments—into flesh." Evan Seinfeld, the bassist for Biohazard, says, "We're all trying to release our negative energy, our frustration with the world. Through our art and our music, we're getting it all out. Shawn Crahan of Slipknot says, "I have a lot of dark ideas in my head. Paul develops these same emotions in very powerful pieces." Booth says, "If I woke up one day and became happy, I probably wouldn't tattoo anymore, because I wouldn't see a need to do it. I would lose my art if I became happy."

"IN SAMOA there is a legend that tattooing was introduced there by the goddesses of tattooing. They swam to Samoa from Fiji, singing on the way their divine message: 'Tattoo the women but not the men.' With constant repetition the message became confused and twisted. When the goddesses finally arrived on the Samoan shore, they found themselves singing just the reverse, and so, says the legend, the tattoo became the undeserved prerogative of the men and not the women."

—Albert Parry

WHO OWNS THESE PARAGRAPHS?

REVELATION 17:5 says of the Scarlet Woman: "And upon her forehead was a name written, MYSTERY / BABYLON THE GREAT / THE MOTHER OF HARLOTS / AND ABOMINATIONS OF THE EARTH."

NBA VETERAN Jud Buechler, now retired, said that Michael Jordan wanted "me and Steve Kerr [Jordan's then teammates] to get tattoos" after the Bulls won their fourth championship. "I thought about it but didn't do it, because I knew my mom, wife, and mother-in-law would kill me."

"THE HUMAN body is always treated as an image of society."

—Mary Douglas

"BY THE EARLY seventeenth century [in Japan], a generally recognized codification of tattoo marks was widely used to identify criminals and outcasts. Outcasts were tattooed on the arms: a cross might be tattooed on the inner forearm, or a straight line on the outside of the forearm or on the upper arm. Criminals were marked with a variety of symbols that designated the places where the crimes were committed. In one region, the pictograph for 'dog' was tattooed on the criminal's forehead. Other marks included such patterns as bars, crosses, double lines, and circles on the face and arms. Tattooing was reserved for those who had committed serious crimes, and individuals bearing tattoo marks were ostracized by their families and denied all participation in the life of the community. For the Japanese, who valued family membership and social position above all things, tattooing was a particularly severe and terrible form of punishment. By the end of the seventeenth century, penal tattooing had been largely replaced by other forms of punishment. One reason for this is said to be that at about that time decorative tattooing became popular, and criminals covered their penal tattoos with larger decorative patterns. This is also thought to be the historical origin of the association of tattooing with organized crime in Japan. In spite of efforts by the government to suppress it, tattooing continued to flourish among firemen, laborers, and others at the lower end of the social scale. It was particularly favored by gangs of itinerant gamblers called Yakuza. Members of these gangs were recruited from the underworld of outlaws, penniless peasants, laborers, and misfits who migrated to Edo in the hope of improving their lot. Although the Yakuza engaged in a variety of semi-legal and illegal activities, they saw themselves as champions of the common people and adhered to a strict code of honor that specifically prohibited crimes against people, such as rape and theft. Like Samurai, they prided themselves on being able to endure pain and privation without flinching. And when loyalty required it, they were willing to sacrifice themselves by facing imprisonment or death to protect the gang. The Yakuza expressed these ideals in tattooing: because it was painful, it was proof of courage; because it was permanent, it was evidence of lifelong loyalty to the group; and because it was illegal, it made them forever outlaws."

—Steve Gilbert

"YOU PUT A TATTOO on yourself with the knowledge that this body is yours to have and enjoy while you're here. You have fun with it, and nobody else can control (supposedly) what you do with it. That's why tattooing is such a big thing in prison: it's an expression of freedom—one of the few expressions of freedom there. They can lock you down, control everything, but 'I've got my mind, and I can tattoo my body, alter it my way as an act of personal will.'"

—Don Ed Hardy

WEREN'T AMERICAN slaves branded by masters to identify them as if they were cattle? I've always thought there was a connection between the gold jewelry worn by rap artists and the chains of slavery—transformation of bondage into gold, escape from slavery, but not quite . . .

DURING THE EARLY Roman Empire, slaves exported to Asia were tattooed with the words "tax paid." Words, acronyms, sentences, and doggerel were inscribed on the bodies of slaves and convicts, both as identification and punishment. A common phrase etched on the forehead of Roman slaves was "Stop me—I'm a runaway."

PETER TRACHTENBERG, the author of *Seven Tattoos: A Memoir in the Flesh,* told me: "The most obvious reason African-Americans didn't get tattooed until recently was that the old inks didn't show up on black skin. Newer, clearer pigments didn't come into use until the mid- to late eighties, which coincides with the introduction of tattoos into the African-American community. I also wouldn't be surprised if tattooing's association with working-class culture—redneck culture in particular—made it unpopular with African-Americans. You don't come across many black country and western fans, either. Charley Pride's fan base is entirely white. My guess is that there were two principal routes of diffusion: the first from rap, the second from black college fraternities (some of which also used branding as an initiation rite). Starting in the late '80s, a number of gangsta rappers adopted tattoos, most notably Tupac Shakur, who had "THUG LIFE" tattooed in block letters down his torso. It would be interesting to go back through magazines of that period and see if photos of tattooed rappers predate those of tattooed ballplayers." They do. "Also, to find out what percentage of NBA players belonged to black college fraternities." Some, but not a lot. "There's some irony at work here. The tattoos mark their wearers as gangstas or gangsta-wannabes, but one of the hallmarks of black gangsta rap is its appropriation of white organized-crime terminology, e.g., the group Junior MAFIA and admiring references to John Gotti in several songs."

"WHITE FOLKS are not going to come to see a bunch of guys with tattoos, with cornrows. I'm sorry, but anyone who thinks different, they're stupid."

—Charles Barkley

A FEW YEARS AGO, the shoe company And 1 created a controversial advertisement in which Latrell Sprewell, who was suspended from the NBA for a year for choking his coach, says, "People say I'm America's worst nightmare; I say I'm the American dream." In the background a blues guitar plays "The Star-Spangled Banner" in imitation of Jimi Hendrix's version of the anthem. (And 1 couldn't afford the rights to the original.) Seth Berger, CEO of the company, said that MTV created a youth market in which blacks and whites are indifferent to color: "It's a race-neutral culture that is open to endorsers and heroes that look different. These people are comfortable with tattoos and cornrows."

WHO OWNS THESE statements—the people who said them or the people who wrote them down or the person who has gathered them together here or the person who reads them?

CONCERNING THE people who are featured in the book *Modern Primitives* and who are devoted to body modification, mutilation, scarification, and tattoos, *Whole Earth Review* said: "Through 'primitive' modifications, they are taking possession of the only thing that any of us will ever really own: our bodies."

IN THE 1890s, socialite Ward McAllister said about tattoos: "It is certainly the most vulgar and barbarous habit the eccentric mind of fashion ever invented. It may do for an illiterate seaman, but hardly for an aristocrat."

UPON HEARING that the NBA's *Hoop* magazine had airbrushed his tattoos off the photograph of him on the cover of the magazine, Allen Iverson responded: "Hey, you can't do that. That's not right. I am who I am. You can't change that. Who gives them the authority to remake me? Everybody knows who Allen Iverson is. That's wild. That's kind of crazy. I personally am offended that somebody would do something like that. They don't have the right to try to present me in another way to the public than the way I truly am without my permission. It's an act of freedom and a form of self-expression. That's why I got mine."

JOHN ALLEN, a Philadelphia high school basketball star, said, "I think that on the court, if I didn't have as many tattoos as I do, people would look at me as—not being soft—but people would look at me as average. When they see me come in with my tattoos and the big name that I've got, before you even play a game, it's like, 'Whoa, this guy, he must be for real.'"

IN THE NINETEENTH century, Earl Roberts, field marshall of the British Army, said that "every officer in the British Army should be tattooed with his regimental crest. Not only does this encourage *esprit de corps* but also assists in the identification of casualties."

WHEN I BROKE my leg as a sophomore in high school, I spent the summer in traction and then in a body cast. The doctor misread the X rays and removed the body cast too early, so I had to have a metal pin inserted to stabilize my left leg. I recently had the pin removed, for no particularly compelling reason of any kind other than it spooked me to think of one day being buried with a "foreign object" in my body (for one thing, it's a violation of Jewish law). Not that I'll be buried; I'll be cremated. Not that I'm religious; I'm an atheist. Still, leaving the pin in seemed to me some obscure violation of the order of things. As one tattoo artist has said, "The permanence really hits other people, and that is linked to mortality. And that is why skull tattoos really ice it."

WHO OWNS THIS body, this body of work?

ABOUT THE AUTHOR

DAVID SHIELDS is the author of three books of autobiographical nonfiction: *Enough About You, Black Planet* (a finalist for the National Book Critics Circle Award) and *Remote* (winner of the PEN/Revson Award); two novels, *Dead Languages* and *Heroes*; and a collection of interrelated stories, *A Handbook for Drowning*. His stories and essays have appeared in numerous publications, including the *New York Times Magazine, Harper's, Yale Review, Village Voice, McSweeney's, Salon,* and *Slate.* He lives with his wife and daughter in Seattle, where he is a professor of English at the University of Washington.